# Ancient Rome

Charles Kovacs

# Ancient Rome

Waldorf Education Resources

Floris Books

First published in volume form in 2005
Third printing 2013

British Library CIP Data available

ISBN 978-086315-482-9

Printed in Great Britain
by Bell & Bain Ltd, Glasgow

# Contents

## Caesars and Christians

## Early History of Britain and the Fall of the Roman Empire

# Foreword

Charles Kovacs was a teacher at the Rudolf Steiner School in Edinburgh for many years. The Waldorf/Steiner schools sprang from the pedagogical ideas and insights of the Austrian philosopher Rudolf Steiner (1861–1925). The curriculum aims to awaken much more than merely the intellectual development– it seeks to educate the whole being of the growing child, that each may develop their full human and spiritual potential.

During his time as a teacher Charles Kovacs wrote extensive notes of his lessons day by day. Since then these texts have been used and appreciated by teachers in Edinburgh and other Waldorf/Steiner schools for many years. This book represents the way one teacher taught a particular group of children, other teachers will find their own way of presenting the material.

There is an introduction written after Charles Kovacs spoke to parents about the purpose of teaching history.

At the beginning of puberty children want to conquer the world around them, just as the Romans did. With an awakening sense and innate feeling for right and wrong, they embrace fairness and justice; logic appeals to them and the just consequences of actions taken, fill them with a sense of satisfaction. In this way the events described in this volume will meet them just where they are at in their own development.

Astrid Maclean, Edinburgh 2005

# History Teaching
## in Waldorf Schools

What is the purpose of teaching children history? It is done in all schools, but that is hardly an answer. It only means that the teaching of history is an established convention but we have to see if this custom is still valid.

In my time I have seen examples of teaching national history with the purpose of implanting patriotism in the hearts of the young. This can be achieved, if you give your teaching a slant in that direction. But this slanted history teaching has been used (and is still being used in some parts of the world) to instil fanatical nationalism and to impart national prejudices. If this were the only aim of history teaching, I believe it would be better for the children to grow up in ignorance of their national history.

Another answer is that a knowledge of history is necessary for an understanding of the present-day world. With this answer we are on more solid ground. But then as far as it concerns the teaching of the *young* – please mark this proviso – history is only important in so far as it is in any way relevant to the present. And, taking this approach, not *all* the ancient kings of Scotland or England, not *all* their battles, wars or treaties, are relevant.

This is our approach to history teaching in Waldorf Schools. It is one of the means to prepare young people for life in the present day. Teaching them the past prepares them for the here and now.

But seen in this light, history becomes a subject of supreme importance. In cases of amnesia, someone may suddenly lose their memory due to a shock or to nervous tension. They have lost the connection with their personal past, they cannot recognise their closest relatives and friends – all are strangers. We are not only separate individuals, but are members of a community, of a nation, of mankind as a whole. And as social beings we need history, just as we need a personal memory as individuals. A person without a knowledge of and a feeling for history is suffering from social amnesia. They meet their own kind as strangers, they are socially without a past. The antisocial behaviour of some young people, their wanton destructiveness, may make one wonder what kind of history teaching (if any) they had at school.

For it is not only a matter of imparting a string of historical facts – it is very much a matter of how this is done. For instance, one of the challenges of history teaching in our schools is to give the children a feeling for time. It does not mean anything to a child of ten if you tell them that Charlemagne lived a thousand years ago. The figure of a thousand years means as little as to the child as millions of light-years of astronomy mean to the layman. It is a great number, but you have not given the child a feeling for time. A kind of graph on the blackboard demands a degree of abstract thought which, in fact, the child does not have until around puberty.

Following a suggestion by Rudolf Steiner, I did the following in my class of children of ten- and eleven-year-olds. I told one child to link hands with his neighbour and said, "Your neighbour is now your father when he was a child."

There was, of course, great laughter in the class. Then I said to the neighbour, "You link hands with the next girl: she is now the grandmother of the first boy."

Then another child joined the chain, the great-grandfather. Now I said, "You see, we have now gone back about a hundred years."

By then, of course, everybody wanted to join the chain as great-great-great-grandparents. And when the whole class had linked hands we had gone back about five hundred years, and the children realised we would need another class of the same size to get back to the time of Charlemagne.

It can easily be seen that such an approach to time contains a social element. The distant past is, then, not a matter of so and so many zeros, but the child feels linked to the past by the classmates who represent his ancestors. This is just a small, concrete detail from our work.

The word "history" and the word "story" are the same. In the German language too *Geschichte* means history as well as a story. And in fact when the writing of history began, in ancient Greece, it was nothing but a collection of stories of great people.

For the child up to the age of fourteen, history must still be just that – a collection of stories. By "story" I mean a tale which speaks to the feelings of the child, a tale which arouses sympathy or antipathy, delight or pity. I don't know if there is such a thing as "objective" history, but if there is, it is not the kind of history that would leave any impression on a young child. Bare, dry facts and dates only bore the younger children, which is worse than giving them no history at all.

And so, in the younger classes, we try to present history in vivid pictures. We try to make the heroes and villains of history as concrete, as real as possible. Nothing is more rewarding for the teacher of children between 11 and 14 than to see a class glowing with enthusiasm for a great deed, or to see a storm of moral indignation on other occasions.

In this way history becomes a moral force. One can try and preach moral precepts to children, but we believe that repeated exhortations and admonitions in the long run produce hypocricy, a false morality that does not spring from the heart. It may also produce outright antagonism against moral authority altogether. But if you can move children to respond with strong feelings to the good and evil that appears in history, then you have laid the foundations of a sound moral sense for life.

Later, between the ages of twelve and fourteen, the child needs already more than an entrancing tale. It is necessary to show connections between events, though not by imposing some hypothetical pattern on history. It is not a thought-out pattern or some hypothesis, if I point out to the children that the change of mentality which found expression in Renaissance art also ushered in the Age of Discovery and erupted in the Reformation.

This brings me to another and quite essential point in our history teaching. It is quite possible to tell a child of ten the story of the discovery of America. There is no difficulty in telling this story in terms which a child of ten can grasp. But for the child of ten the story of Columbus will not be different from the story of

Odysseus – the child is not in any real sense capable of feeling any kinship, any inner relation with the historical situation of Columbus.

It is quite different with children aged twelve to thirteen. At this stage the emotional ties to parents, teachers, to the whole environment have been considerably loosened. The children experience the ability of independent thought, they are eager to find out things for themselves. They become aware of vast prospects that open out before them, vistas which are both attractive and in their vastness frightening, and they feel for the first time the touch of loneliness which comes with the loosening of the childhood ties.

And, at this stage, the outer situation in which Columbus found himself – the break with the recognised learned authorities of his day, the venture into the unknown, the lonely ships in the vast, uncharted ocean – this outer situation corresponds to the inner situation of the child between twelve and thirteen. And if I tell children of this age the story of Columbus (even if some have heard it before) then this story *grips* and goes deeply. It is a *therapy* for the problems of this age.

The lonely researches of Leonardo, anticipating the future, Galileo before the Inquisition, Luther challenging the Church and secular powers, these are the heroes with whom the child between 12 and 13 feels a deep inner kinship. And so history becomes a therapy. The growing child meets his or her own problems, he meets himself on the stage of history.

Let us go a stage further. The following year, age thirteen to fourteen, is usually called a "difficult" age. There are all the problems of puberty, the teenager appears with all his or her unprepossessing characteristics. But what are these characteristics? The young person now asserts their independence, they are highly critical of their elders, but do not take kindly to criticism of themselves. That is one side. Another characteristic is that they do not wish to be treated as children any longer: they want and expect to be treated as equals by adults. At the same time they form close circles amongst themselves: the boys spend time together, the girls form little cliques. This is the age of intensive friendships, the time of huddling together.

At this age the children in our Waldorf Schools come to the time of the French Revolution in history. They hear how great ideals are pronounced, the ideals of freedom, equality, brotherhood. But these ideals are again a counterpart – a historical counterpart on a grand scale – of the forces which work in the young people themselves. Their wish for independence echoes the cry for liberty. Their desire to be treated as "equals" corresponds to the demand for equal rights in the Revolution. Their "huddling together" is the counterpart of the call for universal brotherhood.

In fact, both the ideals and the destructiveness of the French Revolution have their counterpart in the psychological situation of the adolescent, including the self-destruction exemplified by the rise and fall of Napoleon. And so the adolescent meets in the history of this period their own aspirations and their own potential destructiveness, enacted on the vast stage of history. And again this meeting with one's own problems in the guise of history has a therapeutic value, has a healing effect. Of course, it does not eliminate the problems and crises of puberty, but it does make for a comparatively easy passage through this troubled stage.

And then history lessons take the class into the nineteenth century. Here the aspirations, the ideals of freedom, equality, fraternity, arise in a new form. I tell the children of Garibaldi, that fearless adventurer and intrepid fighter for the freedom of Italy. I tell them of Abraham Lincoln who devoted his life to the abolition of slavery and to the assertion of equality, of equal rights for all men. And I tell them of Henri Dunant, the founder of the Red Cross who was inspired, and could inspire others, with a feeling for the brotherhood of all men.

And in this way the ideals of freedom, equality, brotherhood, now arise anew, but not in the form of mass-movements or slogans, but carried by personalities and made real by personal sacrifice and devotion.

Through the Industrial Revolution and its extremes of Capitalism which in the name of freedom offended against the fundamental feeling of human brotherhood. This in turn gave rise to the other extreme, Communism which in the name of brotherhood suppresses freedom. And so the children are led stage by stage to the present day.

At all times and in all aspects, history teaching is never a matter of passing on information, of communicating knowledge just for the sake of knowledge. History is treated as a subject of immense moral and social importance, but also as a therapy, as a healing element for the tensions and problems at each step of the process of growing up.

I would not like to leave the impression that we depend only on history for moral and therapeutic effects. We try in every subject, even arithmetic or science, to meet the deeper needs of the child; here I have taken only history to show in one concrete example the aim of our education.

Charles Kovacs

# From the
# Foundation of Rome
# to the Time of
# Marius and Sulla

# 1. Earlier Civilisations

If we look at the time of ancient India, Persia, Babylonia, Egypt and Greece, and if we take all these stories together, they are, in a certain sense, *one* story, a strange and wonderful story.

In ancient India the five princes, the sons of Pandu, had to leave their kingdom and for a long time live in the forest as hermits. They ate little and devoted their whole mind to prayer. When people prayed so wholeheartedly in ancient India they felt their souls lifted up to heaven, to the gods, and the earth and all things in it disappeared. The people in ancient India wanted to forget the earth.

Just as we sometimes feel homesick when in a foreign country, so the people of ancient India had the feeling that heaven, the realm of the gods, was "home." And while they lived on earth, they were homesick for heaven.

The five sons of Pandu, after many adventures, became kings again. But, after a time, they left their palaces and went in search of the Gates of Heaven. They did not wait for death to take them away from earth, they went of their own will to find the gates of Paradise. It shows how little they cared for life on earth. And the people of ancient India did not care for the body either. When someone died, the body was burned and the ashes thrown into the River Ganges, so that there was nothing left of it.

All this shows that in ancient India people longed for heaven, and did not care much for life on earth; in those very ancient times, about nine thousand years ago, they did not make any useful, practical inventions.

Then we come to another people, who lived later, about seven thousand years ago, the Persians. The Persians also loved the kingdom of light, the kingdom of Ahura Mazda, and the earth was for them the land of darkness, of Ahriman. But they wanted to fight the evil Ahriman, they wanted to fight here on earth for the god of light against the Prince of Darkness.

The planting of crops, of fruit and flowers was one way of fighting Ahriman. To make good things grow, like wheat, fruit trees or roses, was a way of fighting the Prince of Darkness. And nearly all the cultivated plants we grow today come from ancient Persia.

The invention of the plough came to King Jemshid in a dream; Ahura Mazda appeared to him in a dream and showed him a golden dagger. It was the same with all important decisions: they did not try to *think* what was the right thing to do, but waited for a *dream,* and the gods always sent wise dreams.

The Persians of seven thousand years ago were no longer so homesick for heaven; they were already much more at home on earth.

Then we came to the people who lived about five thousand years ago, the people of ancient Babylon. In Babylonia all knowledge, all wisdom was still a gift of the gods, and came in dreams. For instance the art of making bricks was given by the god Ea. And now, having bricks, people could build houses which lasted, and great cities.

While the Persians, the first farmers, had learnt much about the earth, the Babylonians studied the stars, building great towers for observatories. They were the first to divide the day into twenty-four hours and the year in twelve months. Still today we reckon time as the Babylonians did. As well as watching the sun and stars circling the sky, they came to the idea of making a wheel and made the first chariots.

Five thousand years ago the Babylonians were far more at home on earth than the much earlier Indians. But this brought about the feeling that they did not want to leave the earth, and they began to fear death.

The sons of Pandu went in search of the Gates of Heaven without waiting for death, but in Babylonia there was the story of Gilgamesh. When his friend Eabani died, Gilgamesh was so afraid of death that he set out on a journey not to find the Gate of Heaven, but to find the plant of everlasting life on earth. He would have liked to live forever on earth – he was in deepest sorrow when in the end he lost the plant.

The great story of mankind shows human beings at first more at home in heaven and strangers on earth, who look forward to returning to heaven. But later they liked life on earth more and more, and heaven, the kingdom of the gods, seemed to get darker.

Then came the Egyptian civilisation, also about five thousand years ago. The Egyptians did not look for the plant of everlasting life but thought, if they could not live for ever, at least they could preserve the body as long as possible, and keep it as life-like as possible. And so they did not burn the dead like the Indians, but made mummies. They were great builders, not in bricks but in stone, as can be see in the mighty pyramids.

For the Egyptians wisdom still came from the gods in dreams. Remember the Old Testament story of Pharaoh, who dreamed of seven fat cows, and seven lean cows and Joseph who told him what the dream meant.

Wisdom still came from gods, and it was the god Osiris who gave the Egyptians the picture-writing, the hieroglyphs, from which our writing later developed.

And then we came to ancient Greece about 2500 years ago. For the Greeks the kingdom of heaven, the world which the Persians called "kingdom of light," seemed a dark world of shadows. You remember that Odysseus spoke to the soul of his dead friend Achilles, and Achilles said: "I am a king among the dead, but I would sooner be a beggar among the living."

For the Greeks life on earth was beautiful; they loved life on earth and made it as beautiful as possible, as we see in their temples and statues. In the Olympic games, in running, jumping and wrestling, the Greeks enjoyed the strength of their bodies; they loved the human body and the life and strength in it. The Greeks were the first to have theatres and plays; even the word theatre is a Greek word. So in Greece we find the beginnings of arts, sports, theatres; but it was also the time when dream-wisdom came to an end. The Greeks were the first people to think for themselves. Remember Socrates who was such a great teacher of the art of thinking.

In the Persian Wars the Persians were still relying on dreams: it was in a dream that the King of Persia heard a voice that told him to conquer Greece. But the Greeks thought for themselves, and that is ultimately why they could defeat the might of Persia.

The Athenians had no king. Every Athenian wanted to think for himself what should be done in the city and to vote for it. That was the beginning of our kind of government, of democracy (also a Greek word). And through thinking, the sciences began in Greece. History, geography, botany, physics, arithmetic are all Greek words.

And then through Alexander the Great, the thinking wisdom of Greece and the dream-wisdom of the old lands came together in one great empire. Alexander conquered all the countries I have mentioned, Persia, Babylon, Egypt, Greece and even a part of India. He died young, his empire fell apart, but his real aim was achieved. Greek art and Greek knowledge spread everywhere and had made life on earth rich and beautiful.

But – and this is the other side of this great story – the world of the spirit, the kingdom of heaven, had become dark. People enjoyed life on earth, but thought that when they died they would only be shadows in a dark underworld in the kingdom of Hades. And, if nothing else had happened it would have been very sad for all people on earth – how can one be happy on earth if all one can hope for after death is a dark world of shadows?

# 2. Slavery and the Gift of Christ

We have many things today which we owe to people who lived thousands of years ago. From the Persians came the plough, as well as fruit-trees, garden-flowers, wheat and barley. From Babylon came bricks, the first carts and chariots, the knowledge of measuring time. From Egypt came the art of writing, and from the Greeks came arts, theatre, sport, the sciences, and democracy.

The time of ancient Greece already had much knowledge:there were great and wonderful works of art, and human beings had even learned the power of independent thinking, no longer having to rely on dreams.

But even the best and wisest of Greeks thought it quite natural that there should be slaves. For instance, the Spartans were only trained to be warriors, and slaves worked the fields, cooked and served the food. In Athens, the rich Athenians had time to listen to beautiful speeches, to spend days in the theatre, to practice sports, only because all the heavy work was done by slaves. The Athenians had great architects who designed the beautiful temples and who supervised the work, but they did not carry the heavy stones for pillars and walls, they did not cut the stones, all that was done by slaves.

The ships which carried people and goods across the seas had sails, but when the wind came from the wrong direction, or there was no wind, slaves had to row to move the ships. Even warships had to be rowed by slaves. Often these slaves were chained to their benches, so when a ship sank they could not even save themselves by swimming.

All the hard, unpleasant work was done by slaves. Most Greeks treated their slaves well, if only because a slave cost money, and if he was underfed or mistreated he might die, and a new one would have to be bought.

But if a Greek happened to be mean and cruel, he could hurt and beat and even kill his slaves. He was quite free to do so, for a slave was his property to do with as he liked. If a slave ran away he was nearly always caught and condemned to death as a warning to other slaves thinking of running away.

Slaves could only marry with their owner's permission and if they had children these were also slaves, and the owner could take them away from their parents and sell them whenever he liked.

In every city of the ancient world, in Greece, Persia, Egypt, there were slave markets where men and women, boys and girls were sold, just as we sell sheep or cattle or horses. And no one ever thought that there was anything wrong in treating human beings like this. Even the wisest and best people of that time did not have the feeling that here is a fellow human being, just like themselves; they really did not feel it.

An Athenian had a certain feeling of brotherhood with other Athenians – but already a man from Sparta meant little to him, and a man who was not Greek at all, a so-called barbarian, was hardly regarded as human at all. In Greek times and later in Roman times there was no feeling that a human being is something that cannot be bought or sold like a piece of furniture.

But then in Roman times, something quite new came into the world. Christ came and He gave the world the understanding that all human beings on earth are children of the Father in heaven.

We each have our own earthly father and mother, and, perhaps, some brothers and sisters, but we all have one Father in heaven; we come from Him and we return to Him. And through the Father in heaven all human beings are our brothers and sisters and they are all equally dear to Him. That was the precious, wonderful gift given to all children of God. It was the most important thing in the whole of history.

Now that was something so new that many people could not understand it at first, and they even turned against Christ. Even in our time there are people who have not quite understood it and hate and hurt each other. But such great things take time to work, and in time all humankind will understand it.

The gift of Christ has already brought one great change since Greek and Roman times: no one would like to have slaves today. We would feel it as something horrible if there was a slave in our house who would live in fear and dread of us, whose life would depend on our whims and moods. A Greek or Roman would have thought it quite natural. So you see how much life has been changed.

In our time we feel it is against human dignity to have slaves, even if we treated a slave well and with kindness, it would still be wrong. It is against the dignity of a child of God that he should be treated like a pet-dog.

The great painter, Leonardo da Vinci, showed what Christ had given to mankind when he painted the *Last Supper* showing Christ among his disciples, Christ who is so much more than an ordinary human being, Christ who has divine powers, and around Him the men are not his slaves, not his servants. Each one of these men speaks quite without fear. Some are old, some are young, some are excited, some are calm. But the words which Christ says go to the heart of every one of them, different as they are. These men are united by the love of Christ, and not by the command of a master whom they fear because he could destroy them.

So in this picture Leonardo showed the new thing Christ had brought into the world: love for every human being, for we are all children of the Father in heaven, and respect for human dignity, for every human soul is dear and precious to God. One cannot buy or sell a human being who ultimately belongs to God.

We saw that as men learned more and more things to make life on earth pleasant, as they became more and more "at home" on earth, the Kingdom of Heaven became darker and darker for them. For the Greeks and Romans it was already a world of dark shadows. But for those people who followed Christ, all this changed: they could feel the light-filled Kingdom of God near, they no longer feared death, because love and kindness not only brings human beings together, they also bring heaven and earth together. When we love others, when we care for others, the Kingdom of God is in our hearts.

This is why the coming of Christ is the most important event in the whole history of mankind. All the dream-wisdom of the ancient peoples, all the clever thought of the Greeks, all the beauty of Greek art, they are like nothing, compared with what Christ brought. And all the inventions of our time – cars, planes and computers – they are very little compared with the gift Christ brought, because what good would all this be if people live in fear and hatred of each other, if they destroy each other in wars?

But such a great thing as Christ brought takes a long time to grow and to reach all human hearts. Even now we are still far from living like brothers and sisters on earth. And, at first, it was even worse, for the Romans, who came after the Greeks, believed in power and not in love.

# 3. The Latin People

The Greeks had a great sense of beauty. Their temples and statues, even their poetry – the songs of Homer about the Trojan War, about the adventures of Odysseus – still today evoke the admiration of the world. And their clarity of thinking in their philosophy and science, was just as wonderful. But when it came to power the Greeks were not at all skilled; they could never build a great empire. There was, of course, Alexander the Great who conquered a vast empire in a few years, but when he died this empire fell to pieces and each general grasped a kingdom for himself; they were unable to stay together.

The Romans were quite different, they had little sense of beauty, they had no really great thinkers; they had to learn their art and their knowledge from other nations, but they were good at imitating. However, when they came to gain and hold power, the Romans were better and more ruthless than any other nation.

For the beginning of Rome, we have to go a long way back – back to the Trojan War. At the end of this long war, the Greeks gained access to the city of Troy by the clever trick of the wooden horse.

In that terrible night the Greeks fell upon the Trojans and killed them by the thousands. Only one Trojan hero escaped, Aeneas. He could not save his wife who died in the flames, but he carried his old father on his back and led his son by the hand, and with a few servants reached the sea-shore. He found an unmanned ship, and he and his people sailed away leaving the red glow in the night-sky where Troy had been.

For a long time Aeneas and his people sailed the seas in search of a new home. Sometimes they came to islands, barren and empty, where they could not stay, sometimes they came to shores inhabited by fierce warrior people who would not let them stay. At last, after many adventures they saw the coastline of a green pleasant land with many wooded hills, where a warm sun shone. It was the land which we now call Italy.

In those days, more than three thousand years ago, Italy was made up of many little states each with its own king. Now the kings of the part of Italy where Aeneas and his people had landed was called Latinus. And King Latinus received Aeneas with great hospitality and made him welcome, and so he and his people stayed and settled there. In time, Aeneas married the daughter of King Latinus, and, when Latinus died, Aeneas became king of this country.

The name of this hospitable King Latinus is still remembered today, for the language which his people spoke, and which also became the language of Aeneas, is still called Latin.

So it was a Trojan hero, Aeneas, who became king of these people who spoke the Latin language. And when Aeneas died, his son (who was a little boy when they escaped from Troy) became king after him.

And so for a long time kings of Trojan blood ruled over the Latin people. Now one of these kings who descended from Aeneas had two sons, called Numitor and Amulius. When he died, Numitor was the elder son and so, by right, should become king. But the younger son, Amulius, envied his brother Numitor, thinking: "Why should he get everything?" And Amulius complained saying it was not fair and not right that he would not have a share.

Now Numitor, the elder brother, did not want to quarrel with Amulius, and so he said: "I am quite willing to share with you everything our father has left. Tell me, what do you want?"

And Amulius answered: "Well, our father left a great treasure of gold. If you give me the treasure, you can be king and rule the country. But it would not be fair if you both had the treasure and were king."

Numitor agreed, and the royal treasure was given to Amulius. But Amulius had only asked for the treasure because he had his own evil plans to use this treasure in a way his brother had not expected. Amulius secretly made friends with Numitor's bodyguard and gave them gifts of gold, promising them even more if they would do his bidding. When Amulius had bribed the soldiers and had them on his side, he gave them the order to drive out Numitor.

And so one day Numitor was seized by his own soldiers, who took him to a peasant's hut and said: "From now on this is your palace." They showed him a herd of sheep and said: "You can rule these sheep from now on."

And so the cunning Amulius set himself up as King of the Latin people. But this was not enough: he had to make sure that no one would one day claim the throne. King Numitor's daughter, Rhea, was not a danger to Amulius, but if she had sons they might one day be a threat. So Amulius had Rhea taken to a temple and imprisoned there. She was locked up, a woman brought her food only once a day, and no man saw her in that temple. Now at last Amulius felt safe.

But Amulius had made his plans without thinking of the gods. And this was still a time when gods sometimes appeared in human shape and took sides in human quarrels, as they had done in the Trojan War.

And there was one of the gods who now took sides, and that was the god of war and strife and battles. The Roman name of this god was Mars. In pictures they showed him with helmet and armour, sword and shield and a body of enormous strength and power, and with a black beard and eyes that struck fear into all who saw him. But this god, who enjoyed the clash of arms, the wild noise of battles, and the steady step of marching soldiers, was no friend of cowards like Amulius who had gained power by a mean trick.

It was Mars who appeared to Rhea in the temple where she was imprisoned and comforted her, and in time, he became her husband. Rhea bore him two boys, twins. Soon the god Mars said: "I can hear in far away countries the sound of war-drums and of trumpets calling men to battle, I must leave you, for I must be where men seek victory or death. But fear not, Rhea, whatever may happen, our twin sons will not come to harm by anything that the evil Amulius can do."

And so Mars, the war-god, departed. But Amulius came to

know that Rhea had given birth to sons. He was furious, and made up his mind to destroy the children before they could become a danger to him.

From the very beginning there is little kindness or love in Roman history – there is no wise Pallas Athene, only the fierce god of war.

# 4. Romulus and Remus

Before we go on with the story of the sons of Rhea, we shall look at life in those ancient days in the sunny land of Italy. There were still dense, trackless forests on the hills, and there were wild animals, bears and wolves. Only in the winding valleys between the mountains were there fields of barley and corn. The peasants and shepherds built their little houses not in the valley, but on a steep hillside. You might think this made it very inconvenient every time you had to go from your house to your field and back, down hill, up hill, but a village on a hill-side was harder to attack when enemies came. And such attacks were quite frequent, the people living in one valley often raiding the sheep or cattle of a village in the next valley.

In the forests there were not only bears and wolves which killed many a sheep or cow, but there were also bandits and robbers in the forests. If a man in a village had committed a crime, he often ran away before he could be punished and joined the lawless bandits in the forests. The herdsmen who took the cattle and sheep from one grazing to another had to be armed to drive off wolves as well as gangs of robbers. So fighting was natural, it was part of life to these people.

The "cities" were only slightly larger villages built on a hill and surrounded by a wall. The houses were simple cottages, and even the house of the king was not a palace but just a larger cottage with a big hall. The city where King Amulius lived, Alba Longa, was of that kind.

Amulius had driven his brother Numitor from the throne to live as a peasant, and Numitor's daughter had been imprisoned in a temple and had borne twin sons whose father was the fierce war-god, Mars. Amulius decided that these babies had to die so that they could not turn against him when they were grown up.

And so Amulius gave the order that the little boys should be taken from their mother and thrown into the nearest great river, the Tiber.

The servants went to the temple where Rhea was imprisoned. They paid no attention to her cries and tears, but seized the children and carried them away. To make it easier for them to carry the babies they put them in a basket, and so they came to the River Tiber.

At that time there had been much rain and the River Tiber had risen and flooded its banks, and the servants could not get near the main stream of the river. So they threw the basket with the children into the nearest flood-water, and then left. But the River Tiber was kind to the babies, for soon after the servants had gone, the flood began to recede and the basket was left high and dry on the banks.

There was a cave nearby that was the den of a she-wolf and her young wolf cubs. And the she-wolf came to the river at night to drink. She heard the wailing babies and came to the basket – she took first one baby and carried it to her den – and then the other. And in the den the she-wolf suckled the two human babies together with her own cubs.

So it came, that these two brothers lived for a time on wolf's milk. Wolves are wild creatures and some of the wolf's nature may have come to the children from living on wolf's milk.

But there came a day when the she-wolf was out of the cave, perhaps hungry for food for herself, and a shepherd passed by the cave. He heard the children's voices and the yapping of wolf-cubs and looked inside. And there he saw the two boys and picked them up and took them home to his wife. They had no children of their own and they were grateful to the gods for having found two strapping little boys whom they could bring up as their own. And they called one boy Romulus and the other Remus. So it came that Romulus and Remus grew up as the sons of the shepherd.

These two boys, when they grew up, were even fiercer and tougher than the other young shepherds on these wild hills. Once when a gang of robbers came from the forest, drove some herds away and also took some shepherds as prisoners, Romulus and Remus went after them, killed the robbers in a furious fight, and set their friends free. From that time onwards Romulus and Remus became leaders of the hill-shepherds, who would do anything these two young men asked.

In those days it was quite usual to take other people's sheep, and Romulus and Remus took some sheep that belonged to the herd of Numitor, who was the grandfather of Romulus and Remus. Now Numitor was already an old man, who could not defend himself against raiders. But the other people of that little hill-city Alba Longa did not like what had happened; next time these raiders might come for their sheep. So some of them hid in the hills and when Remus was by himself they fell upon him, bound him and brought him before old Numitor.

Numitor looked at the young man; he should have felt angry, but strangely enough, he could not feel angry; quite the contrary, he liked the young shepherd. And another strange thing was that the youngster had a noble manner and bore himself more proudly than any simple shepherd. So Numitor asked that Remus' father should be brought to him. And then he heard the whole story how the two brothers had been found in the she-wolf's den. Now Numitor knew that this young man was his grandson. And he embraced him and welcomed him as his grandchild.

But in the meantime Romulus had heard that his twin-brother had been taken prisoner, and he was not going to stand for it. He called his shepherd friends, and they all came fully armed and followed him to Alba Longa to free Remus. Amulius, the evil king of Alba Longa, heard that a crowd of furious shepherds were coming towards the city. He armed himself and his soldiers and they rushed out, thinking it would be easy to deal with these rough men from the hills. But they were mistaken, it was a furious battle and in the fight Romulus slew Amulius. And as soon as their king fell, the soldiers fled in all directions.

Now Romulus and his shepherds stormed through the city gates to find Remus and set him free. Imagine their surprise when Remus and old Numitor came to meet them. And great was the joy when Romulus heard that he and his brother were the grandchildren of the rightful king. They rushed to free their mother, Rhea, from her imprisonment in the temple. Now Numitor was again placed on the throne that was his by rights, and the people of the city and the shepherds celebrated together with a great feast.

But Romulus and Remus did not wish to stay in the city of Alba Longa. They wanted to build a city of their own, a city on the hills where they had roamed as shepherds, a city on the bank of the River Tiber that had saved their lives. They did not know yet that only one of them was to rule that new city.

# 5. The Foundation of Rome

Romulus and Remus decided to build a city of their own. It should be near the River Tiber that had saved them, and it should be on top of a hill. But there were seven hills to choose from, and the two brothers could not agree which of the hills it should be. On the advice of their grandfather, King Numitor, they agreed that the gods should decide where the new city should stand. It was done in this way: Romulus went to the hill he liked best, and Remus climbed to the top of the hill he preferred. Then each of the brothers built a little altar of stones, made a sacrifice and prayed to the gods. Then they both looked up and watched for a flight of birds, for the gods would show their will by sending a flight of birds.

And so each on his hill watched keenly, waiting for what they would see. Suddenly Remus called out: "I see a flight of birds, six of them, they are flying over my hill!" He had hardly finished when Romulus saw another flight of birds coming over his hill – but they were twelve. According to the ancient rules, this made Romulus the winner, for his birds had been more.

For hundreds of years this remained the custom. Important matters were decided by flights of birds. Not only the numbers of birds were taken into account, but the direction from which they came, whether they flew high or low, what kinds of birds they were. People would not start on a journey, generals would not go into battle, ships would not sail, unless they had first let a flight of birds tell them if things would go well for them or not. Foretelling the future by birds was called *augury* and, in later times, there were special people called augurs, who did nothing else but tell people what this or that flight of birds meant, it was a special science.

But in the case of Romulus and Remus, it was quite simple: Romulus had seen more birds, so he had won. The new city was to be built on the hill he had chosen, which was called the Aventine Hill. Now the other brother, Remus, was not very pleased but he had to give in, for the augury had decided for Romulus. But he soon had more reason to be angry.

Romulus called all his shepherd-followers together on this Aventine Hill and said: "The gods have decided that here a city shall be built where you shall live. But who shall be king of this city, I or my brother?"

And they all cried: "You, Romulus, you shall be King!"

Romulus said: "So be it. And it shall be called Rome."

Now Remus had always expected he and Romulus would both be kings, they would share the power, and he was full of bitterness that Romulus had made himself alone master of the new city. But Romulus took no notice of him. He set about preparing the building of the city and just ignored his disappointed brother.

In those days you did not start a new city by just building houses. No, it was quite a ceremony. First Romulus dug a deep hole in the ground and into the hole he threw a handful of wheat-grains, and every one of his men threw a little earth on it, until the hole was filled again. This was done as if to say: "May the city never want for food." Then a white cow and a white bull were yoked together to a plough, and Romulus drove them round in a wide circle, that was to be the boundary of the city. And while he did this he prayed to the gods that his city, Rome, should grow strong and mighty. And, as if in answer to this prayer, there was thunder and lightning in the sky.

And when the boundary was marked on the ground by the furrow of the plough, the men began to build a wall where the mark was. The city wall was the first thing, for in those days you first had to think of enemies who might come and attack, and no house would have been safe unless it was within the protection of walls.

The founding of Rome, the day when the building of Rome began was April 21, 753 BC (according to other sources 747 BC). This city, whose boundaries could be marked by a plough, in time grew from one hill-top until it covered seven hills and became the capital of an empire that reached from Scotland to Egypt. This vast empire began with a little fortress-city on a hill.

When Romulus and his men began to lay the first rows of stones for the walls of the future city, Remus, who had watched the ceremony of ploughing with bitterness, could not hold himself. He jeered at their work and made jokes about the wall. This annoyed Romulus. Of course, the wall was still very low, only the first rows of stones had been laid and Remus kept on saying: "What a mighty wall this is, what a wonderful protection for the city of King Romulus."

Romulus grew more and more angry, and Remus became more pleased: it was one way of paying his brother back for making himself sole king without sharing. And then Remus jumped over the wall and cried: "See how these walls protect the city!"

Now Romulus lost his temper, he drew his sword and struck his brother, and Remus fell down dead. And Romulus looked down on his dead brother and said only: "So shall everyone perish who tries to get over the walls of Rome."

So the very day of the foundation of Rome, the first day in the history of Rome, was a day of bloodshed. Romulus killed his twin brother.

As the walls grew higher, the shepherds who had chosen Romulus as king, began to put up their houses inside the walls. But there were not many of them, while the space inside the walls was big enough for many more, and so most of the city was still empty.

But Romulus wanted a city full of people, he wanted a large number of men whom he could rule and who would obey him. What could he do to increase the number of his followers? There were the outlaws, the bandits and robbers who had their hide-outs in the hills and forests. These men could never return to their own cities or villages for if they did they would have been put to death.

Romulus offered asylum, a safe refuge, to every outlaw, robber, murderer, which no other city or village wanted. They were *invited* to come and settle in Rome. And from all over Italy they flocked to Rome in their hundreds and filled the city. Here they were protected against any punishment which their evil deeds had earned them.

So the first king of Rome was a man who had killed his own brother, and the first inhabitants, the first citizens of Rome, were bandits and robbers, thieves and murderers.

# 6. The Sabine Women

At the founding of Athens the sea-god, Poseidon, and the goddess of wisdom, Pallas Athene, competed for the honour of becoming protectors of Athens. Poseidon gave a horse and Pallas Athene gave the wonderful gift of the olive-tree. That is quite different from the story of Rome that begins with bloodshed between brothers. And the the first inhabitants of Rome were not men with a great sense of beauty, but were robbers and worse.

Romulus had as many men as he wanted – men who had lived for years by their strength and by their cunning – but there were not enough women. Few girls and few wives had lived in the robbers' dens in the hills, and so these men had come without womenfolk. But once they were settled in Rome, they wanted wives and families of their own. But when they went to the villages and cities in the neighbourhood and asked for girls to marry, they were driven away with scorn, for no father wanted his daughter to go and live with these outlaws. In those days it was the parents decided whom a girl should marry.

The men complained to King Romulus, what was the use of being citizens of Rome if they could not have wives, children, a family? Romulus saw that the outlaws would not stay with him unless they could get wives. So he decided on a ruse to get what he wanted.

There was a tribe living not far from Rome, peaceful people, called the Sabines. The girls of these Sabines were famous for their beauty. Now there came the time of a great harvest festival and Romulus sent messengers to the Sabines and invited them to come with their families on that festival day and watch the games and races in Rome.

And the Sabines all came with their womenfolk and they were received with great hospitality. They were given food and wine and then the games began. There was wrestling and races and other displays. Suddenly, at a sign by King Romulus, armed Roman warriors rushed in among the guests and seized the Sabine maidens and, despite their screams and struggles, carried them away. The Sabine men had come in peace, unarmed; they could do nothing to help their daughters. They hurried away from the treacherous city of Rome, but they swore they would come back and punish this city of robbers.

But Rome, set on a hill and surrounded by strong walls, was not a city that could be stormed easily. The Sabines – who were really peace-loving people – took two years to prepare themselves for fighting the fierce Romans. After two years, they were well-armed and ready to march against Rome. Even then they would hardly have breached the walls manned by the fierce Romans, if there had not been a traitor among the Romans, a traitor who was a girl. Her name was Tarpeia. This girl had seen that the Sabines wore golden arm-bands on their left arms, and she loved gold more than anything else in the world.

One night she came to the Sabines and promised she would open a gate in the wall for them if the Sabines would reward her with the bands they wore on the left arm. Then she stole back to Rome. Next day the Sabines stormed the walls of Rome, and the defenders on the walls showered a hail of stones and arrows upon them. Suddenly a gate opened, and the Sabines rushed in.

By the entrance stood Tarpeia, the girl who had betrayed her own people. She cried: "Give me my reward, the things you wear on your left arm!" But the Sabines despised traitors – even a traitor who had been useful to them – and they threw what they wore on the left arm at her. They were not the golden bands, but their heavy shields, and Tarpeia was killed by the weight of them. Then the Sabines picked up their shields and stormed into the city, and there was wild fighting in the streets of Rome.

Now the Sabine maidens, who were the cause of all this fighting, had in the meantime married Romans. They had grown fond of their husbands and they had borne them children. And now, there in the streets, these children's grandfathers and fathers were fighting and killing each other. The

Sabine women could not bear to see this happen. With their babies in their arms, they rushed between the two fighting armies, they threw themselves between the fighting men with loud cries to end the slaughter.

And they held up the babies who stretched out their arms as if they too were begging for peace. The Sabine warriors had rushed into Rome, furious to revenge themselves, but now at the sight of their daughters who had stepped fearlessly between clashing swords, who begged on their knees to end the bloodshed, at the sight of the children held up, their own grandchildren, the mad fury of revenge and battle went from them, and the Romans too lost their will to fight.

One after another they dropped their weapons, the Sabine fathers embraced their daughters, they clasped hands with their former enemies the Romans, and they lifted their little grandsons and granddaughters proudly on their shields. The battle ended in peace and friendship between Sabines and Romans, and they became one people. This battle between Romans and Sabines is the only battle in history that was not won by either side, but by the women who never fought at all. Even the women came to Rome only by force, by a trick. For once, an evil deed ended in peace and friendship, the Sabines and the Romans became one people, under King Romulus.

Romulus ruled for forty years, and then a strange thing happened. In the city there was a great open field, called the Field of Mars (Mars was the god of war and the father of Romulus and Remus). Now Romulus ordered a great assembly of all people on the Field of Mars for a festival. But when they were all together a terrible thunderstorm broke. Thunder rolled, lightning flashed, winds howled, torrents of rain poured down, and the clouds darkened the sky so that it seemed like night. The people ran in terror from the field and fled to their homes. When the storm was over and the sky was clear again, Romulus, the King, had disappeared and no one ever saw him again. The Romans said he had been taken from earth by his father, the war-god.

The next king who was chosen to rule Rome was a man from the Sabines, a man of peace, of wisdom and justice. His name was Numa Pompilius, and during his reign there was no violence, no bloodshed, no war, the fields gave food in abundance, the herds of cattle and sheep grew, it was a time of peace and prosperity for the young city. But after this peaceful king, there came other kings and they brought war again.

# 7. The Etruscans

In these early days of Rome life was very simple. The men worked in the fields or with their flocks, the women spun wool and flax into yarn and the yarn was woven on looms into cloth. They made their own pots and pans from clay.

A Roman house of that time was very simple. It had only one room where all the members of the family lived together. The house had no windows but a hole in the roof through which light came in. There was an open hearth in the corner, the fire in it was never allowed to go out and the smoke of the fire escaped through the hole in the roof. When it rained the water that came through the hole was caught in a bucket.

There was no writing, no books, no paintings or statues, there was even no money. At the foot of the hill was the Forum, the market-place, where the Romans exchanged sheep for grain, or cattle for wool.

But not all people in this part of Italy were as simple as the Romans. To the north of the River Tiber there lived people called Etruscans who were much more civilised than the Romans. Like the Greeks, the Etruscans had a love of beauty. They had beautiful frescoes of dancers and musicians. They also made statues, not from stone like the Greeks, but of clay which was then heated and hardened in a kiln. They were skilled metalworkers, making beautiful ornaments in gold, silver, bronze. They were merchants whose ships carried goods to Greece, Egypt and Persia, Babylonia.

Compared to the Etruscans, the Romans were "barbarians." But the Romans wanted to learn from these civilised neighbours to the north. So Roman kings had Etruscans as teachers of their children, and as advisers in all matters of government. And when the Roman King Ancus died, the Romans chose an Etruscan as their next king.

In the time when Etruscan kings ruled Rome the kingdom grew and spread. Instead of one hill where Romulus had built his city, Rome spread out over seven hills, and ever since Rome was called the City of Seven Hills. Some of these seven hills can still be sees today in Rome, but others are so built over that they are barely visible. But the River Tiber that once saved the lives of Romulus and Remus still flows through the city of the seven hills.

Under the Etruscan kings Rome became a great city, and the Romans learned many things. They built better and bigger houses, they learnt writing, and they began to use coins for money. The Romans were never much good at inventing things for themselves, but they were very good at imitating the skills of other people. And from the Etruscans they learnt a great deal.

The Romans were quite happy under these Etruscan kings, as long as these kings ruled wisely and justly. But the last of these wise kings, Servius Tullus, was murdered by his son-in-law. He would have become king in any case when Servius Tullus died, but he did not want to wait years until his father-in-law died a natural death, so he had him stabbed to death, and became king, an evil and cruel king. His name was Tarquinius, but he was called Tarquinius Superbus that means Tarquinius the Proud.

Of course the people of Rome were horrified that a man who had murdered his father-in-law should rule them, but any-body who spoke openly against Tarquinius was seized by his soldiers and executed. And if a Roman was wealthy, there was the danger that Tarquinius would take a liking to his house, or his fields, or his treasure, confiscate his goods and kill him. If he was poor, Tarquinius made him work like a slave, and if he did not work hard enough he lost his life.

But it was not only Tarquinius himself whom the Romans hated and feared. He had two sons who were just as bad as their father. They used to ride through the city and if people did not get out of the way quickly enough, they were struck with horse-whips. And if they saw something in a shop or a house which they liked, they simply walked in, took it and rode away laughing.

Servius Tullus, the old king who had been murdered by

Tarquinius, had some relatives – brothers, cousins, nephews. And Tarquinius feared that of these relatives might revenge the murder, that one of them might lead a rebellion against him. And so one by one these relatives were seized and put to death. Only one of them was spared, one of the old king's nephews. This young man, knowing that his life was in danger, pretended that he was not in his right mind, that he was a half-wit. When people talked to him he would stare at them and then, suddenly, burst out laughing without any reason; sometimes he would mumble to himself, or he would fall on his face without any reason.

The Romans called him Brutus, which means "dull-witted," somebody who has no more sense than an animal. We sometimes say of an animal "this poor brute," or we speak of "brutal" treatment when people are treated like animals. These words "brute" and "brutal" come from "Brutus," somebody who has no more sense than an animal. Because this young man, Brutus, seemed to be so foolish and dull, King Tarquinius thought he would never be a danger and let him live.

The Romans had learned a great deal from the Etruscans, they had become more civilised, but now, under Tarquinius, they paid a terrible price for it. They had to live under a cruel tyrant and no life was safe.

# 8. The Republic of Rome

The Etruscans were skilful people who had a sense of beauty, creating paintings, statues and beautiful metal ornaments as well as being excellent builders. The Romans, who were good at copying, learned much from the Etruscans. One thing they learned, which the Greeks had not known, but which the Etruscans had invented, was how to build an arch. The Greeks made doorways with a flat lintel across the opening, but the Etruscan arch could even be built in the round to make a dome.

Another thing the Romans learned from the Etruscans was writing with the letters of the alphabet, but this was something the Etruscans had learned from the Greeks. The Etruscans had strange ways of foretelling the future. A priest would kill a sheep on an altar, and then he would open the dead animal and look at the heart and the liver of the sheep, and from the condition of these organs he would foretell whether a journey or a business would go well or not.

But the Etruscans – and the Romans who imitated the Etruscans – regarded with special awe, fear and respect certain women who lived by themselves in a forest cave, or on a hill, far from other people. These women were called *sibyls*, and it was said that knowledge of the future came to them from wind, clouds, storms. Such a sibyl lived away from other people and only rarely did she leave her cave. At the time of King Tarquinius, that evil tyrant, a sibyl left her mountain cave and came to the king in Rome. She was old, so old that no one could remember having seen her as a young person, but she stood as straight as a pine-tree and she was so tall that she seemed to tower above other people. A veil covered her grey hair and she carried nine books.

And she spoke and said to King Tarquinius: "In these books

is written the future of Rome. I will sell these nine books to your for a thousand pieces of gold."

But King Tarquinius, who was mean and greedy, cried out: "That is far too much money for nine books."

And the sibyl said: "Do you think so?" And she took three of the nine books and threw them into the fire that was burning in the hearth.

"There are now six books left," she said, "and for these six books I still want a thousand gold coins."

"Never," cried King Tarquinius.

Then the sibyl took another three books and threw them into the fire. "These are the last three books in which the destiny of Rome is written," said the woman, "and they still will cost you a thousand pieces of gold."

And now Tarquinius was frightened of the woman, even a king would not have dared to rouse the anger of a sibyl – and he paid for the three books the price for which he could have bought all nine. The books were placed in a temple and whenever Rome was in danger the priests consulted the books to find if there was a way to save the city. But the books of the sibyl told King Tarquinius nothing about his own fate – perhaps this was something that had been written in the books the sibyl had burned. And King Tarquinius was worried about his future; at night he was haunted by terrible dreams, he saw the father-in-law and the other people he had murdered and he could not find peace by day or night.

One day he made a sacrifice to the gods in a temple and suddenly a snake came and devoured the sacrifice before his eyes. The king thought this could only mean danger and evil for himself. He was so alarmed that he decided to ask of the most famous place for prophecy in the world, the oracle of Delphi in Greece. He sent his two sons and Brutus, the nephew of the old king, the young man who pretended he was not in his right mind.

The three had to travel by sea and by land and at last they stood before the priestess in the temple of Delphi and asked her what it meant that a snake had eaten the sacrifice of Tarquinius. And the priestess said: "It is an evil omen indeed, it means that the reign of King Tarquinius will soon come to an end."

"Who shall rule after him?" asked the princes.

The priestess answered: "He shall rule who first kisses his mother."

Now the two sons of Tarquinius were in a hurry to get back and to race each other to their mother, but Brutus understood the real meaning of the words of the priestess.

As soon as they left the temple, Brutus pretended to stumble and fell in his face – and the others had seen this stupid fellow doing that kind of thing before, but they did not see that this time he kissed the earth, he kissed mother earth, and that was the mother the oracle had meant. The priests had a kind of secret language among themselves; in that language heaven was called the father, and earth was called the mother. We ourselves are children of heaven and earth, for our spirit that lives for ever, comes from heaven and our body comes from earth. Brutus knew all this and kissed mother earth, while Tarquinius' two sons only thought of their own mother. But from that time onwards Brutus began to have secret talks with other Romans who were willing to rise against the evil king and his sons.

There came a time when King Tarquinius was waging war against another city in Italy, and his two sons were with him. But one of his sons left the camp to treat himself to some rest from fighting and to enjoy himself in Rome. On his way he passed the country-house of a Roman officer who was away serving King Tarquinius. But the officer's wife was at home, a beautiful woman, called Lucretia. The prince stopped at the house of Lucretia and was made welcome by her. But the prince looked at her and thought: "I could do with such a beautiful wife." And the sons of Tarquinius always took what they wanted. So he told Lucretia that she had to come with him. Lucretia refused, but the prince only laughed and dragged her away. She could not fight against a strong man, and in her despair she grasped a knife and plunged it into her own breast.

Tarquinius' son simply rode away, leaving Lucretia dying. She was still alive when her husband came back a few hours later and could tell him with her last breath what had happened. Then Brutus came too and heard from the husband the terrible tale.

They took the body of Lucretia to the Forum, the market place, in Rome. And there, before thousands of Romans, Brutus spoke. He told them what had happened – it could happen to any of them as long as they let Tarquinius and his sons rule Rome; but the time had come to make an end of this rule. And his fiery words roused the citizens of Rome who had suffered so long. They swore that neither Tarquinius nor his sons should rule again, and they took up arms to fight against Tarquinius. And the soldiers who were with Tarquinius heard what had happened to one of their officers, and they deserted him and joined the rebels.

Tarquinius and his sons, now abandoned by their soldiers, fled to their own people, to the Etruscans. But the Romans decided that never again would they be ruled by a king. Rome became a republic. Every year two men were chosen, two men who for one year had equal power to rule, to make laws and to see that justice was done in the land. These men were called Consuls, and the first two Consuls of the Roman Republic were Brutus – and Lucretia's husband Collatinus.

So it was that Brutus, who was supposed to be stupid, had freed Rome from the tyrant Tarquinius.

# 9. How Horatius Kept the Bridge

Rome was the city of seven hills, having grown from the one hill where Romulus had built his walled city until it covered seven hills along the River Tiber. But it was also a city of seven kings: the first king was Romulus himself, then came the peaceful Sabine king, Numa, followed by two Roman kings, Tullus Hostilius, Ancus Martius; and finally there were three Etruscan kings, Tarquinius Priscus, Servius Tullius and Tarquinius Superbus. And the third Etruscan king, cruel Tarquinius, was also the seventh and last king of Rome.

Tarquinius had been driven from Rome and had fled to his own people, the Etruscans. But he was not a man who would give up so easily. He persuaded an Etruscan ruler, Lars Porsena, to take up arms and march his army against Rome.

It was Brutus, the first Consul, who led the Romans against the Etruscans. The two armies clashed in a furious battle. At one point Brutus saw one of Tarquinius' sons. He spurred his horse forward and aimed his spear, and so did the Etruscan prince. They rode so furiously against each other that they pierced each other with their spears and both were killed and fell from their horses.

The Romans won this battle, but it was a sad victory, for they had lost Brutus. They chose another Consul, Valerius, to take his place. But the Etruscan king, Lars Porsena, was thirsting to revenge the defeat and soon marched again against Rome.

Once more the Romans went out of the city to meet the Etruscan foes in open battle, but this time they were beaten, and they fled in haste back to Rome and behind them came the Etruscans. And where they passed the Etruscans burned down the villages and homesteads in the countryside around Rome.

Just outside the walls of Rome there was a little hill, called Janiculum; it was connected by a strong wooden bridge to the walls of Rome, and beneath the bridge there rushed the mighty River Tiber. The Romans tried to make a stand on this little hill; they tried to hold the Etruscans, but it was in vain: the Etruscans stormed the hill.

Now the Consul, Valerius, and the other leaders inside Rome were in a desperate position. The Etruscans could easily attack Rome by coming across the bridge, so the wooden bridge had to be destroyed. But it would take time to break it down. Who was going to stand on the other side, on the hillside of the bridge and fight off the Etruscans until the bridge was destroyed? And, of course, once the bridge was destroyed, the men fighting on the other side would not be able to return.

But Romans never lacked courage. A soldier who had lost an eye in a battle, came forward and volunteered to hold the Etruscan army long enough that, behind him, the planks could be thrown down. And once this brave man, Horatius, had offered himself for this desperate task, two of his friends, Spurius and Herminius, volunteered to come with him. Fully armed, the three men hastened to the end of the bridge on the Janiculum hill and shouted defiance at the approaching Etruscans.

The Etruscans, as many as they were, could not all attack at the same time, they would have been in each other's way. Only a few Etruscans could attack at one time, and, Horatius in the middle, his friends on either side, fought like lions; they held the Etruscans at bay and the dead foes lying in heaps before them made it even harder to get at them.

Behind them their fellow-Romans heaved the great planks and beams of the bridge and let them crash into the water of the river deep below. When they were at the last beam they cried out to the three fighting heroes: "Come back quickly!"

Horatius' two friends quickly turned and darted back over the swaying beam. But Horatius stayed on to fight until not a single piece of wood was left. As Horatius struck down another enemy, there was a mighty crash and the last beam fell down into the Tiber.

Now he stood quite alone, facing thousands of enemies and the bridge behind him had gone. Bleeding from many wounds he called out, "Father Tiber, River of Rome, take care of a Roman's life!"

Then he hurled himself down into the river. The Etruscans in their fury threw their spears after him, but none of them reached the bold swimmer. Several times Horatius went under, dragged down by the weight of his armour, but each time he came up until reached the other bank where helping hands were ready to drag him to safety.

Horatius' heroic deed was forever remembered in Rome. Lars Porsena and his Etruscans could not take Rome by storm once the bridge was gone, and after a time he made peace with Rome. Tarquinius gave up all hope of regaining the kingship and died friendless and homeless.

Many years later the Romans conquered one Etruscan city after another, the conquered Etruscans became Romans, and in time even the Etruscan language disappeared. Today we know only that they were skilful builders and artists, who taught the Romans many things, and that they did not speak Latin. There are inscriptions but no one now knows what the words mean.

Only from Roman writers do we know that there were once Etruscan kings ruling in Rome and that the last, Tarquinius Superbus, was driven out when Rome became a Republic.

# 10. Patricians and Plebeians

Tarquinius, the seventh and last king, had been driven from Rome. The Etruscans had not only been driven off but had themselves been conquered by the Romans, and the city of Rome was no longer a little fortress on the hill Romulus had chosen, but a great city spreading over seven hills. It had become a Republic, ruled by the citizens, not by a king.

The streets in the city were very narrow, there were no pavements. Pedestrians, donkey-carts piled with fruit or vegetables, horse-riders, were all crowded into these narrow lanes. The houses were low, but many temples on marble pillars towered above them. A visitor from Athens would soon have seen that the Roman gods were the same as the Greek ones, but with Latin names.

There was a temple for the sun-god, Apollo, and a temple of his sister, Diana, goddess of the moon, and also of hunting as well as the protector of children. There was the temple of Mars, the war-god (closed in rare times of peace) and the temple of Venus, the goddess of love (Aphrodite in Greek). There was the Temple of Mercury, the god of trade and business (Hermes in Greek). High on the Capitoline Hill, one of the seven hills, was the Temple of the "father of the gods," Jupiter (Zeus in Greek). In French you still hear the Latin names of these gods in the days of the week *(mardi, mercredi, jeudi, vendredi)*.

At the foot of the hill on which the great Temple of Jupiter stood was the great market-place, the Forum. But the Forum was a market-place only once a week. Every seven days the peasants from the countryside came in to sell grain, meat, vegetables and fish. There were also stalls selling honey in combs which was used to sweeten food because sugar was still unknown.

Once a week there was the crowd, the shouting of peasants acclaiming their wares, the men and women bargaining and haggling for their shopping. On other days the Forum was much quieter, but it was important for another reason.

Imagine a visitor from Athens coming to that great open place, the Forum on a quiet day, and a Roman would explain to him what he saw: "The man over there, followed by two slaves, is wearing a tunic, and over the tunic, draped over the left shoulder, he has a large white woollen cloak called a toga. We Romans take great pride in our togas. They are worn by men and women, the rich use fine, soft cloth, the togas of the poor are of coarse material. Young children wear only the tunic – and it is a great day in the life of a Roman boy or girl when, at a great ceremony, at the age of fourteen, they are given their first toga. But the slaves only wear a tunic – they are not allowed to wear a toga. The man I showed you, the man with the fine beautiful toga, he is a patrician."

The visitor from Athens, curious, asked: "What is a patrician?"

And the Roman replied: "The first people who settled in Rome may have been shepherds and robbers, but since these olden days, the grandsons and great-grandsons of these first Romans have become rich and powerful. And because these families are the oldest in Rome, they are called 'father-families,' patricians [Father in Latin is *pater*]. The other people who came later when Rome grew over seven hills. They are quite poor; we call them the 'common' people, or *plebeians*.

And the Roman man continued: "In a Roman home, the father is absolute master, his wife and his children obey him without question, they would not even dream of arguing or disobeying him, and he even has power of life and death over them. He could sell them as slaves. And as the father is the master of his family, so the 'father-families,' the patricians, are the masters of Rome. From these old families, these noble rich and respected families, the Senators are chosen."

"Who are the Senators?"

"The wisest, most experienced patricians are chosen to be Senators. *Senex* is the Latin word for old, and these Senators are all people who have seen many years of life before they are considered wise enough to become members of the government, for these Senators are the real government of Rome, they are the fathers of the city. When we drove out Tarquinius we swore we would never have a king in Rome again. Instead of this we are ruled by the senate, the gathering of Senators.

"When our soldiers march into battle they carry standards on which is written: SPQR which stands for *Senatus populus que Romanus,* the Senate and the people of Rome. Our public buildings too bear this inscription. And all our laws are given in the name of the Senate and the people of Rome. We are very proud of having this kind of government, but like so many other things – writing, building, the use of coins for money – we have copied it from the Etruscans. Here on the Forum is the great Senate where the Senators meet."

Then the Athenian visitor asked: "But what happens when there is a war? These elderly men of the Senate could not very well lead soldiers into battle."

"No, but the Senators choose two young patricians as Consuls. These Consuls are our leaders in wartime, and when there is peace they see to it that there is law and order in Rome. These Consuls have great power – but only for a year. Then the Senators choose two other Consuls from the young patricians, and so no one has power too long."

"And who are your soldiers?" asked the Athenian.

"Every Roman citizen between the ages of seventeen and forty-five, who is in good health must be ready to serve in the army as soldiers whenever we call him, whether he is a noble patrician or just a common plebeian. The patricians are the officers of the army and ride and fight on horse-back, the plebeians are the common soldiers and march and fight on foot."

"Are the plebeians, the common people, satisfied that they have no say in the government? From the patricians the Senators are chosen, the Senators pick the Consuls from the patricians, that does not give the plebeians any say at all. Nor can they become officers and leaders in the army."

"Well," said the Roman, "there has been some trouble from time to time. Once the plebeians even walked out of the city and threatened to build a new city of their own on a hill outside Rome. But they were persuaded to come back, for – in the end

– the plebeians are just as proud to be Romans as the patricians and whenever there is an enemy to fight (which is most of the time) then we forget our squabbles and arguments and fight side by side. For we all, patricians and plebeians, have only one wish and one desire, to make our city of the seven hills the greatest, richest, most splendid, most powerful city in the world."

And the Athenian said: "I wish my own people in Athens would think like that! Although we have more beautiful temples, greater artists, wiser teachers than you, we shall never become as powerful as you Romans will be one day in the future."

# 11. Roman Laws and Ways

The Romans had something which the Greeks did not have. What was it? The Roman father was absolute master in the house: the mother and the children obeyed his every wish and command with absolute obedience, both in small things and in bigger matters. It was the father who decided when his son or daughter should marry: no young Roman would have thought of making their own choice.

From their early youth Romans were used to obedience, and to discipline. Even the word "discipline" comes from a Latin word, *discipulus* which means somebody who has to learn, or a pupil. Being used to it from childhood, the Romans kept discipline right through their life. In the home, the father laid down the rules and everyone obeyed. In the state the Senate laid down the rules, and everyone obeyed.

Once a law was made, the Romans thought it should never be changed. That is why the laws and rules of the Senate were always carefully written down. When a Roman Consul had to pass judgment, say between two sons who could not agree how to share their dead father's property, the Consul would not think, "What is the fairest way of sharing out the possessions in this case?" but he would look up which laws had been written down long ago, and would decide accordingly.

While the Greeks would change laws after a time, the Romans did not; they stuck to the written letter of the laws. The Romans believed in justice, but it was a dead justice that did not come from the heart but from old books.

When a Roman Consul walked through the streets to give judgment in court, twelve men called *Lictors* marched before him. They carried bundles of wooden rods surrounding an

axe, the head of which stuck out from the bundle. These
bundles, called *fasces* were the signs of Roman justice. All
people in the street respectfully made way for the Consul
who wore a special toga, edged with purple. And every child
in Rome knew what this bundle meant: the Consul could
have wrongdoers flogged with rods or have them beheaded
with the axe.

Being so used to strict rules from their childhood, the
Romans also kept a harsh discipline as soldiers in their army. A
man who did not obey his officer, an officer who did not obey
his general, a general who did not obey the Senators, lost his life
without mercy.

But, being trained under this strict discipline, the Romans
became better soldiers than any nation of their time. Over his
tunic a Roman soldier wore a breast-plate of metal, held by steel
bands. A metal helmet protected his head. He carried a large,
carved shield made of strong wood with a metal rim and an iron
knob in the middle. For weapons he carried a six-foot spear and
a short two-edged sword.

In a battle, the Roman soldiers fought in three lines. The
first line, the front-line, were young soldiers who had as yet
seen little or no fighting; the second line were soldiers who
had already fought a good many battles; and the third line were
soldiers who over the years had seen so much fighting and
been in so many wars and battles, that it was just a part of life
for them.

So if in some battle the soldiers of the front line, to whom it
was all new and terrible, lost their nerve, there was the second
line of more experienced men to stop the enemy. If they too
wavered and gave way, there came the last line, the soldiers to
whom the noise of battle, the whistle of arrows, the clash of
swords, and the cries of the wounded and dying, were as famil-
iar as the noise of a busy road is to us. These were the men who
would stand and die fighting and would not turn and run. The
soldiers of this last line were called veterans from the Latin word
*vetus,* which means "old, experienced."

When the Romans attacked they first threw the long spears
until the enemy's line was broken, then they charged and in the

close, man-to-man fighting the short sword was used with deadly skill.

The Roman army was divided into regiments or legions, each of about five thousand men. At the head of each legion was the standard-bearer (they had no flags or banners) with his standard of a bronze eagle on a pole, and the proud letters SPQR.

Every Roman from the age of seventeen to forty-five, whether patrician or a plebeian, had to serve as a legionary, a soldier, whenever he was called up by the Senate. Sometimes the Senate wanted many soldiers, sometimes only a few legions were needed, but every Roman had to be ready to go to war for Rome.

And, ever since the time when Horatius held the Etruscans at bay on the bridge, Rome was fighting war after war to increase its dominion. Italy was made up of many small states, and the Romans conquered these little states one after another, until the whole of Italy was under Roman rule.

In the southernmost part of Italy the Romans came up against Greek cities, which had been founded by Greeks who had settled in Italy. Naples was such a Greek city. These Greek colonies were wealthy, flourishing cities of merchants whose ships sailed the seas and carried goods from one land to another. The profit from this sea-trade had made these Greek cities rich.

The Romans conquered the Greek cities in Italy, as they had conquered the rest of Italy. But the Roman conquerors looked with admiration at the works of art of these Greeks, at the temples and statues, they admired the learned men with their wisdom and knowledge. They learned from them as much as they could, and imitated them. As they had earlier learned from the Etruscans, so they now learned from the Greeks.

Originally the Romans had been mainly peasants, knowing very little of business, and even the use of money they had learnt from the Etruscans. But now they learned from the Greek cities in Italy that rich profits could be made from the sea-trade, from sending out ships which bought goods in one place and sold them at a higher price somewhere else.

Soon Roman ships were sailing the seas, bringing Rome
wealth and treasure.

But this brought against Rome the most dangerous enemy
she had as yet encountered, a city older than Rome, as mighty as
Rome, a city which had also grown rich by the sea-trade and did
not want Roman competition. This city in North Africa was
called Carthage.

# 12. Carthage

The sea around Italy is a great sea surrounded by land. The Romans called it the sea amid land, *Medi-terra*(nean), the Mediterranean Sea. From the most ancient times this sea has been like an enormous highway on which not only goods and people travelled in the sailing-ships but also knowledge. The Egyptians and Greeks had sailed the blue waters of the Mediterranean for trade and conquest.

But the most fearless sailors and the most cunning traders of them all were the Phoenicians. It was the Phoenicians who simplified writing by developing the alphabet, which in turn was taken up and changed by the Greeks.

The Phoenicians had their homeland on the coast of what is now Lebanon, north of the Holy Land. As their ships ranged far and wide over the Mediterranean, they built their cities wherever there was good trade. Their largest city, Carthage, was on the coast of Africa, just opposite Italy. Over many hundreds of years Carthage had grown to be a city of wealth and power. Each Carthaginian merchant's house was like a palace built from marble and rare wood, with immense gardens, and a multitude of slaves looked after the master and his possessions. The temples of Carthage gleamed with gold, but the gods worshipped in these temples were not the gods of Greece. The gods of Carthage were cruel gods and human beings were sacrificed to them.

The merchants of Carthage were rich and powerful with vast treasures of gold and precious gems in their cellars. And so rich were they that they did not even fight their own wars, but paid others to fight their battles for them; and so well did they pay that Greeks, Egyptians, Persians and Africans came to serve as soldiers in the great city of Carthage. Only the highest officers and generals were Carthaginians. All the soldiers were foreigners who served and fought for the money they were paid, they were mercenaries.

Now the merchants of Carthage did not like it at all that more and more Roman ships now sailed the Mediterranean and took away their trade. Nor did they like to have such a powerful neighbour as Rome just across the Mediterranean. The Carthaginians thought it was high time to crush the Romans, and the Romans, of course, thought it was about time to finish the city of Carthage and to make themselves masters of the Mediterranean.

And so war began between Rome and Carthage, a war that was fought on sea and on land; but for a long time neither side could gain victory, and even when they made peace for a time, they lived in fear of each other.

The greatest of the Carthaginian generals was Hannibal. From childhood he had only one aim in life, and that was to conquer Rome. Hannibal was still a little boy when his father, Hamilcar, a great general of Carthage, took him into a temple of the Carthaginian god Baal and said: "My son, I want you to swear before the statue of this god, our highest god, that all your life, whatever happens to you, you will hate Rome and the Romans, that you will fight against them as long as you live." And the nine-year-old boy raised his right arm and cried out: "I swear by the gods of Carthage that as long as I live, I shall hate and fight Rome and the Romans."

From that day onwards Hannibal went with the soldiers of Carthage wherever his father went. He sat with his father's soldiers at the campfire at night, he helped them sharpen their swords and polish their armour. He listened eagerly when they came back from battle speaking of the furious fights and of enemies they had slain. He listened eagerly when his father and other officers made plans for the next battle. The mercenaries, the paid soldiers of Carthage, liked the plucky boy. They let him handle their weapons and ride their horses, and they taught him skills with sword and spear. So Hannibal grew up among soldiers and looked forward to the time when he would himself be a soldier and a leader.

When Hannibal's father died in battle, it only made Hannibal more keen to become a great general like his father. Eventually he became the Commander-in-Chief, the highest general of Carthage.

Up to this time, the Carthaginians had made their attacks against the Romans only in one way: they put their soldiers in ships, landed them on the Italian coast, and then they had tried to fight their way to Rome, but they had always been driven back.

But then Hannibal, now commander of the armed might of Carthage, had a dream. (And this shows that the people of Carthage still had dream-wisdom, and had not learned yet to think as the Greeks had.) In his dream he saw the Mediterranean Sea and the countries around it from high up, like a map. And Hannibal saw a fiery dragon that came out of Carthage, crawled along the coast of Africa and into the land which was called Iberia (now Spain), and crawled through Iberia into Gaul (France) and then it turned and came to enormously high mountains, the Alps. But the dragon did not stop; it crawled up the mountains on one side and down the other side into Italy, into the land of the Romans. And now where it crawled, the dragon breathed fire and, one after another, the cities of Italy went up in flames.

And then Hannibal awoke. And he realised that the dragon he had seen in his dream was to be his army, and that he should invade Italy by marching his troops through Iberia and Gaul and across the Alps and so come into Italy by land from the North, not by sea from the South.

# 13. Hannibal Crossing the Alps

The Phoenicians were fearless sailors and clever traders. For example, tin is a very useful metal; when mixed with copper the mixture is called bronze, which can be shaped and formed into helmets, shields and breast-plates for armour. It is very hard and has a beautiful almost gold colour. Copper was mined in the island of Cyprus in the eastern Mediterranean, and so the people who lived around the Mediterranean did not have far to go for their copper. But tin was rare, only a little could be found in a mountain here and there.

But the Phoenicians found an island inhabited by wild people far in the North. On this island tin could be mined in great quantities from the hills. In exchange for tin the Phoenicians offered the natives, who were only dressed in animal skins, red cloth and white linen. And they sailed back with shiploads of tin which they could sell at a good price to the Greeks, Egyptians and Persians. This island in the North was Britain, and the tin came from the tin-mines in Cornwall.

Carthage was a Phoenician city whose ships sailed the seas, and whose merchants could pay foreign mercenaries to fight their wars for them. As long as the Romans were farmers and herdsmen, the merchants of Carthage were not troubled, but when Roman ships began to sail to Egypt, to Greece and to Iberia, and took away trade and business from them, it had to be stopped. And the Romans, for their part, wanted all the sea-trade for themselves. The wars – there were three wars between Rome and Carthage – were wars over trade and profit. The Romans called these three wars the Punic Wars, *Punic* being the Latin word for Phoenician.

The first of the Punic Wars was indecisive. The Carthaginians could not ship a large enough army to conquer Italy, nor could the Romans cross over to Africa and conquer Carthage. It was

Hannibal, who as a child had sworn to fight Rome as long as he lived, who in a dream saw that the best way to get into the Italy was from the North.

The Romans never thought that their enemies might come from there because the North was cut off by a chain of mighty mountains, the Alps. Even in summer the summits of these mountains are covered with snow, ice and glaciers. It was hard enough for a single traveller to make his way through a pass between the towering heights, for there were no roads, and the valleys were inhabited by warlike mountain-tribes who rolled rocks and boulders down onto any intruders who were fool-hardy enough to pass through their land.

But Hannibal gathered an army of a hundred thousand mer-cenaries from every part of the world: there were skilled swords-men from Greece, cunning archers from Persia, Africans who threw stones from slings with such force that they could shatter a man's helmet and skull, there were men who drove chariots with long curved knives on their wheels which cut down any-body who stood in their path. And there were forty trained war-elephants, who could use their trunks to strangle enemies, their enormous legs to trample down whatever stood in their path, and who could carry towers with archers on their backs.

With this mighty army and his forty elephants Hannibal set out, following the path which the dragon had shown him in his dream. Along the coast of Africa they went, crossing where Africa and Iberia are close together, which in those days it was called the Pillars of Hercules, now the Straits of Gibraltar. In Iberia (Spain) city after city surrendered, terrified by the might of his army, and gave them all the food and help they wanted. On they marched northwards crossing the mountain range of the Pyrenees. And then they came into Gaul (the country we now call France). The natives were a Celtic people who hated the Romans, and were only too glad to help Hannibal and his army on their passage through Gaul. And so the great army of Hannibal reached the foothills of the Alps. It was already late in the year, it was October and snow began to fall.

Now most of Hannibal's soldiers came from warm, sunny lands and had never seen snow before, nor had they ever seen mountains of such terrific heights. Even the boldest among Hannibal's soldiers looked with awe and fear at the towering heights, at the white, icy peaks. But they trusted Hannibal, their leader, a man who had grown up among them and who would share every hardship with them.

So the ascent began. They had to make their way along narrow tracks, so narrow that there was just room for one man or one animal. The whole army was stretched out in one single line moving upwards, panting and sweating even in the ice-cold air.

On one side of these rough tracks the cliffs rose steeply like walls, on the other there yawned precipices so deep that the men dared not even look down. By that time the track was already slippery with snow. The horses and, specially, the elephants were quite unused to this kind of road. And so, ever and again, an elephant or a horse would slip, lose their foothold and crash down the precipice taking a few men with it. The others could only watch in helpless horror, seeing their friends and beasts dashed to pieces on the rocks far below.

The air became thin, and so cold that it seemed to cut like a knife; as soon as a man stopped to catch his breath and give his weary limbs rest, he was shivering and shaking with the cold. The soldiers became so worn out, so downhearted by the strain and bitter cold that they just flung themselves down and wanted to die rather than go on.

But it was Hannibal's courageous spirit which made them move on again. He seemed to be everywhere; here he talked like an old friend to a man shivering in the cold wind and encouraging him to go on, there he helped another man, weakened by exhaustion, to get over a dangerous rock, and somewhere else he calmed a horse frightened by a falling stone.

And so the great army struggled on upwards. Then to add to their troubles, the wild mountain-tribes lay in ambush for the men. They hid on the slopes above the track, and when a line of soldiers passed below them, great rocks and boulders came rolling down hurtling them down the precipice. Hannibal gathered his strongest men to storm the slopes and drove the wild mountain-people away. (The descendants of these mountain-tribes are the Swiss.) At last the army reached the highest point of their climb, and from the heights they could see, stretching far below, the plains of Italy.

"Look, my men," cried Hannibal, "there before you lies Italy with all its riches – and all these riches will be yours!"

But they soon discovered that the way down was, though shorter, worse than the way up. Now every path and every track was deep in snow. A soldier would suddenly sink into a deep snowdrift and disappear forever. Another one would step on a thin layer of snow which hid a deep crevasse in the ice and fall down the hole and break his neck. Or an enormous avalanche would come hurtling down and bury a whole company of soldiers, and bar the way for the others. And the soldiers all suffered terribly from frostbite, and a good many even died of it.

Hannibal's army reached the valley, the terrible heights of the Alps were behind them, the whole crossing had only taken ten days, but there were only thirty thousand men and twenty elephants left. The men were exhausted, worn out and suffering from frostbite. Yet two days later they had to go into battle against a Roman army.

No one but Hannibal could have made these tired men, who had no time to recover from the terrors of the crossing, go into battle against a Roman army that was fresh, well-rested and bursting to destroy these impudent invaders.

# 14. *Hannibal Ante Portas!*

While Hannibal marched his army slowly through Iberia, the Romans had not been asleep. They sent a fleet of their soldiers to Iberia to stop Hannibal, but they came too late. Hannibal was already in Gaul. And when the Romans heard that Hannibal intended to come into Italy across the Alps they thought he had gone mad. His troops would be so weakened by the terrible journey that it would be child's play to destroy them.

So the Roman army went back to Italy and waited in the North, at the foot of the Alps, for Hannibal's army. They rested and had a good time while Hannibal's troops struggled over glaciers and snowfields.

Only two days after the crossing Hannibal's exhausted men, still suffering from frost-bite, had to face twice their number of well rested Roman soldiers who were eager to fight. There were sixty thousand Romans against thirty thousand men of Carthage. The Romans had been told by their general, Scipio, that victory against the worn-out invaders would be child's play; they went into battle cock-sure that their enemies would not put up a good fight. But Hannibal's men took heart and gained courage from their general who by his words and example made them fight like lions. The Romans were surprised by the fighting fury of their enemies and they were terrified by the elephants. They gave way, retreated and fled. Hannibal had won his first battle.

A second battle, shortly afterwards, went the same way. Now the whole of northern Italy lay open before Hannibal. Cities and villages simply surrendered. In Rome itself, the people could hardly believe the announcement at the Forum that this terrible invader, Hannibal, had twice defeated Roman armies. He had to be stopped, for soon Rome herself would be in danger.

A great Roman army was gathered – peasants had to leave their fields, artisans their shops, patricians their villas. Rome was in danger and every healthy Roman man had to come to the defence of his city. A mighty Roman army of a hundred thousand under a Consul, Flaminius, marched north against Hannibal. This Consul was a rich businessman with little knowledge of warfare, while Hannibal was the greatest general since Alexander the Great.

Hannibal with his thirty thousand men caught the Romans in an ambush near a place called Cannae where the road passed between a hill and a lake. Hannibal's men lay in ambush on the slope of the hills, and when the whole of the Roman army was well inside the trap, they came down on them like an avalanche.

A sudden hail of javelins, darts and stones from slings burst upon the Romans, killing hundreds and creating terror and confusion among the others. Then Hannibal's soldiers came charging down, their faces half-concealed by the visors of their helmets, the legs protected by greaves of bronze, the shields as low as their knees, the whole troop moving like one, shield alongside shield. On either side of these foot-soldiers came horsemen, pointing their lances between the ears of their horses. And behind this first wave of attackers, came the elephants, their trunks painted red so that they looked like writhing serpents, their chests armed with spears, their tusks lengthened by blades of steel. The elephants had been intoxicated with a mixture of pepper and wine and they trumpeted wildly.

Among the Romans there was utter confusion. Clouds of dust rose, so they could barely see. The uproar was terrible: above the voices of captains, the blare of clarions and the cries of the wounded, came the clash of swords and the whistling of arrows and stones.

Encircled on all sides, hemmed in by their own men, confused and terrified, the Romans were slaughtered like cattle, cut down by swords, trampled down by elephants. Many were pushed into the lake and drowned, weighed down by their armour. Only about a quarter of the great Roman army escaped. The others, including the Consul, died at Cannae.

It was the worst disaster that had ever happened to the proud Romans. In all their history the battle of Cannae was never forgotten. When the news of the battle was announced in the

Forum, a loud cry went up from the people, the cry: *"Hannibal ante portas!* Hannibal is at our gates!"

Many of the people began to prepare themselves to flee from the city. But one of the Senators, Fabius, spoke to them: "Romans, do not forget that to lose a battle is not the same as losing a war. Our second Consul, Varro, still has enough soldiers to defend our city when Hannibal comes. If we stand together in this time of trial we shall still defeat the invaders from Africa." And, in the end, he persuaded the Romans not to give up the struggle.

As it happened, Hannibal was in no hurry to attack Rome herself. Although his own officers urged him to march on Rome, he refused. He said: "My soldiers have done wonders, they have won every battle, but we are not strong enough to take Rome. Winter is now coming and by next spring the men will be rested and more soldiers from Carthage will join us. Then we will take Rome. But now, for the winter, I want to take the whole army to a pleasant city in the warm South of Italy where they shall have a well-earned rest."

And so for a whole winter Hannibal's soldiers enjoyed a life of ease and pleasure in Capua, a lovely, sunny place. They feasted, ate and drank, were served by slaves, and lived a life of luxury and comfort. While Hannibal's soldiers grew soft and lazy under the blue sky and flower-scented air of Capua, the Romans trained and worked and planned for the battles they would have to fight in the spring.

# 15. The Destruction of Carthage

When Hannibal's soldiers came down from the icy heights of the Alps they had been worn out and tired, but in spite of this they had again and again defeated Roman armies much larger than their own.

Now for many months they had enjoyed a well-earned rest of leisure and pleasure in sunny Capua. But the easy life in Capua had made them soft and lazy, and they no longer had the right spirit for long marches and hard fighting.

The Romans, however, had made good use of the winter-months: they had formed new legions – even young boys of fourteen and fifteen had been made soldiers – they had trained hard, and they were in the right spirit to fight. The Romans were led by Fabius who had rallied the people of Rome when they were in despair.

Hannibal realised that the soldiers he had with him could not march on Rome. He hoped for a new army that was to come to his aid by sea from Carthage. And a new army did come, led by Hannibal's brother, Hasdrubal, but the Romans attacked the new army before they could join Hannibal, and this time it was the Romans who gained victory. Hannibal's brother and thousands of his men were killed in the battle, and thousands more were taken prisoners.

Without new troops to help him, Hannibal could do nothing. So for a time there was no great battle in Italy – because the Romans were quite satisfied to let Hannibal hold a small part of Southern Italy – he was no danger to them any more. And Hannibal, for his part, could not risk a great battle with the Romans. The Romans had a saying at that time: "Capua was Hannibal's Cannae."

In the meantime the Romans were busy in other parts. They conquered the whole of Iberia (Spain and Portugal) and sent a fleet of ships to the north coast of Africa. There they landed a large army that marched on Carthage. Now that was very clever, for Hannibal could not stay in Italy when his own city, Carthage, was in danger. The elders of Carthage called him back. And so Hannibal and his soldiers left Italy and sailed home to Africa. It was a sad day for Hannibal when he saw the shores of Italy disappear. He had come with high hopes to crush proud Rome, but nothing had come of them.

Back in Africa, Hannibal soon led a strong army against the Romans. As well as his veterans, the soldiers who had crossed the Alps with him, he had mercenaries who were proud to fight under the great general, and he also made Carthaginians themselves go and fight for their country. Additionally he had a large number of elephants.

But the Romans were always quick in learning new things, and they had discovered that loud noises upset the elephants. In this battle the Roman Consul, Scipio (the son of Scipio who had lost the first battle against Hannibal in Italy) gave the order that a great number of bugles, clarions and trumpets should be blown. It was a terrific uproar and noise and it frightened Hannibal's elephants so much that they turned and trampled down his own men. There was terrible confusion, so much confusion that mercenaries and Carthaginians fought each other. Then the Romans swooped down on the confused enemies and killed thousands, while the rest fled; Hannibal himself escaped, but this day, this battle of Zama, was a bitter day for him, for he had been beaten by the hated Romans.

After this terrible defeat at Zama, the people of Carthage asked Rome to make peace. Carthage had been so weakened by the wars that she could no longer be a danger to Rome; Iberia was now in Roman hands, so no army could come that way into Italy, and so they made peace with Carthage. The Romans wanted Hannibal to be delivered to them, for they were still afraid of him. But Hannibal fled from Carthage before he could be taken.

Hannibal now become a mercenary, a man who served any

king who would pay him. Of course, he would not be a common soldier, but a leader. He went to Greece and became general of a king there, but the Romans soon demanded of that king he should deliver Hannibal to them. Hannibal was warned in time and fled to another Greek ruler, King Prusias. Again Romans came and demanded his surrender. By that time every city and every ruler in Greece feared the power the Rome, and Hannibal knew there was no one who would risk a war with Rome for his sake.

But Hannibal – the proud victor of Cannae, the man before whom Rome had trembled and had cried in fear, "Hannibal at our gates" – was not going to give the Romans the pleasure of marching him in chains through the streets of Rome, with crowds jeering, scoffing, and pelting him with stones before executing him.

And so he said to the King Prusias: "I know you cannot refuse to hand me over to the Romans. But the Romans shall not rejoice to see me as their prisoner. I have a ring which contains a deadly poison, and I will sooner die by this poison than by Roman swords. By this poison I shall die, and with me dies all hope for Carthage, my dear home. Carthage is doomed, as I am." And with these words he put the ring to his mouth, and fell down dead.

That was the death one of the greatest generals of all time. And what he had said about Carthage also came true. For when, in time of peace, Carthage again became wealthy, the Romans could not bear to see their old enemy flourish. They declared war, and this time there was no Hannibal to stop them.

Carthage was not only defeated, the city itself was taken by the Romans and all the inhabitants taken prisoners and sold as slaves. The rich merchants of Carthage who had been served by hundreds of slaves now became slaves themselves. But this was not enough. The walls, the houses and villas, the temples of Carthage were all razed to the ground, they were all destroyed until there was nothing left but the bare ground. Then ploughs drawn by oxen were driven over the site where Carthage had been, and salt was thrown into the furrows. This was to say: nothing shall grow where Carthage used to be. Much later, a

Roman city was built there, but of ancient Carthage, the city of Hannibal, nothing was left.

Rome alone was now master of the whole Mediterranean Sea. There was no longer any country around this sea that could stand up to Rome, and in time Greece too became a Roman dominion.

# 16. A Patrician's Home

Once Carthage had been completely destroyed, there was no longer any country on the coast of the Mediterranean Sea that was strong enough to resist Rome. About five hundred years after Romulus had ploughed a furrow to mark the site of his city, not only Italy, but Iberia, the whole of Greece, Carthage and its coast, and the coast of North Africa opposite Greece, had all come under Roman dominion.

All these conquests changed life in Rome. From the tribute of the conquered lands and from the trade of Roman merchants wealth poured into Rome. From Greece the Romans took the most beautiful statues and paintings and brought them to Rome to adorn the Forum and public buildings. There was no patrician who would not have some great work of art from Greece in his house.

Greek teachers, Greek doctors and Greek artists were greatly admired in Rome, and they gladly came to this wealthy city where the Romans eagerly learned from them. One could really say: the Roman sword conquered Greece, but Greek knowledge and Greek art conquered Rome. When a Roman writer composed a poem it was sure to be an imitation of Greek verse.

Not all the people of Rome had become rich by these wars and conquests. Most of the plebeians had lost what little they had. A plebeian peasant who had a little plot of land outside Rome, was called away from his land into the army for years. His wife and children could not work the land, so they would sell it to a rich patrician and could then live from the money, but when that was finished, there was nothing.

In the meantime the patricians bought slaves; slaves were cheap – all the prisoners taken in the wars were sold as slaves – and there were plenty of them. Now slaves worked the land. So when the plebeian peasant came back from the wars there was no farm, there was not even work for him on the land, and he and his family could starve or beg in the streets of Rome, or sell their children as slaves, for they had nothing else to sell.

So the plebeians had not gained anything by the wars; on the contrary they were worse off than before. The patricians had become richer, but the plebeians had become poorer.

In Rome at this time (about 150 years before the birth of Christ) there lived a noble lady, a patrician lady, whose name was Cornelia. She was a widow and she devoted herself to bringing up her two young sons, Tiberius and Gaius. She and her children lived in a beautiful house, like many a wealthy Roman family.

That house was quite different from any kind of house we have now. Cornelia's house had no garden in front or behind, but was built in a square surrounding a garden, or rather a big courtyard. The front part of the house, the part facing the street had no living rooms at all. It was let to shopkeepers. Between the shops was the entrance. Walking through the entrance you came into the garden with a green lawn, flowers, two or three fountains flowing, and gleaming white marble statues.

On the right and left side of the garden were the rooms of Cornelia's many slaves. They were lucky slaves for nowhere in Rome were slaves treated better and with more kindness than in Cornelia's house.

Walking on through the garden you came to the largest and most important part of the house. Coming inside from the garden you entered first an enormous wide hall called the atrium – every rich person's house had such an atrium – and the walls of the atrium were painted in beautiful colours.

In the middle of the atrium there was a big pool of rainwater which came through a hole in the roof. The roof was specially built to catch the water, sloping inwards towards the hole, not outward like our roofs. Living in a hot climate, the Romans liked to see the rain fall into the pool of the atrium.

In the atrium the lady of the house, Lady Cornelia, would come and welcome you. And then she would lead you to a curtained-off part of the atrium. This part had curtains all around it, from ceiling to floor, and was the dining room. A slave would hold the curtain open for people to enter the dining room.

This dining room was quite unlike any dining room in our houses. There was an enormous table but no chairs. Instead of chairs, on three sides there were long couches, and one side of the table was left free. So you did not sit down for your meal, you lay down on your left side, leaning on your left arm, and using your right hand to help yourself to the food. And the side of the table without a couch was where the slaves served the food and took the empty plates away.

There were no spoons, knives or forks at all, there was no soup in a Roman meal. The meat was cut by slaves into chunks and you took the chunk with your hand; after every course another slave brought a basin with water and a towel to wash and dry your hands. Another slave would mix wine with water (Romans and Greeks never drank wine unmixed) and fill your cup. Before you took your first sip you would spill a few drops of the wine on the floor – that was a kind of sacrifice to the gods.

You would have found a Roman meal heavy going: several kinds of meat – veal, pork, lamb, a meat pie – fish, chicken or peacock, and bread to go with it, but no vegetables of any kind. Then some sweet cakes (all made with honey) and fruit. (Of course there were no potatoes, no tea, no coffee).

After the meal, Cornelia might have taken you to the children's room where the two boys, Tiberius and Gaius, were taught by Greek and Roman teachers. There you would have seen what the Romans used to write on. Papyrus was expensive and was only used for important things. If a Roman wanted to send a short message to a friend – for instance, "Can I come and see you tomorrow afternoon?" – then he used a square of beeswax in a wooden frame. He had a little metal stick that was pointed at one end and flat on the other. And with the point of this stylus he scratched the message on the tablet.

There was no postal service, so he had to send a slave with the message to his friend. The friend would write under the message, "Yes, you will be welcome," and the slave brought the wax-tablet back. Then he wiped out the whole writing with the flat part of the stylus, smoothed the wax so that it could be used again. Children who practiced writing in Latin as well as in Greek would also use these wax-tablets, for cheap paper such as we have today did not exist.

Another interesting thing in a Roman house, was how they kept it warm in winter, without stoves. The floor in the living rooms, atrium and bedrooms was raised on little pillars; it was not on the ground. Outside the wall of these living rooms there was a wood fire and the smoke from this fire was led through a hole in the wall under the floor. This kept the floors and the whole room warm. The idea of under-floor heating, this very modern idea, is a very old Roman idea.

# 17. The Plebeians' Tenements

The great and beautiful house of the noble lady, Cornelia, stood on the slopes of the hill where once Remus had seen the flight of six birds. This hill – one of the seven hills of Rome – was called the Palatine Hill, and all the other houses on the Palatine hill were patrician houses, the houses of noble, rich families, with large courtyards, sprinkling fountains, gleaming with marble.

So beautiful were the patricians' houses on the Palatine hill that the Romans called any beautiful house anywhere in the world, a Palatine house, a house that could stand on the Palatine. And from this came the word "palace" which means a house worthy to stand on the first hill of Rome.

But Cornelia wanted her two boys to know that there were also other houses in Rome, the houses where the poor, where the plebeians lived. So one day she took them for a walk. From these gleaming villas, kept spotlessly clean by the many slaves, from these great house high up on the Palatine, they went downhill.

At the foot of the hill they came first to the Forum. There Cornelia pointed out to her boys the many temples with their shining pillars and the statues of the gods and heroes, many of these had been brought from Greece. She showed them the rostrum, the stone platform from which Senators, Consuls and other important people used to make speeches to the people, and she showed them the great Senate where the Senators met, the patrician elders who ruled Rome.

Cornelia said, "In this Senate the laws of Rome are made, and we Romans are very proud of our laws, of our justice. We boast to other people of Roman justice and of the books in which the rules of justice are laid down. But now I am going to

show you something which is not fair, not just at all, something
that should make us proud patricians ashamed."

They left the splendid Forum, and came to a part of Rome that
was not on the hillside, but between hills. It was damp, marshy
ground, and on this unhealthy ground stood the houses of the
plebeians. These were tenements, similar to blocks of flats. The
ground floor of such a house was built of bricks, but the next two
floors (they were no higher) were made of wood. The rooms in
these houses were small and the ceiling so low that you could
barely stand upright in them. Whole families, often with eight or
ten children, lived in one such room. The rooms were filthy, and
so were the people who had to live in these little spaces. They did
their cooking, eating, sleeping, all in one room.

The streets between these houses of the poor were so narrow
that even the bright sun of Italy could not bring much light into
the houses. The windows were not of glass, but just holes in the
wall. The people in the streets wore togas so dirty and ragged
that they looked like sacks. And these streets were not paved: in
the dry weather you walked ankle-deep in dust, in rainy weather
you could hardly move in the thick mud.

Between the grown-ups dirty children darted. At night-time
these streets were pitch-dark, for there was no street-lighting,
and the rooms too were in darkness, for the people could not
afford oil for their lamps.

You can imagine that the two boys, coming from the beautiful home on the Palatine, shuddered at the sight of this kind of
life. But their mother, Cornelia, said: "You should know that
many of these men you see in rags have fought bravely for
Rome in Iberia, in Africa, in Greece. The one-armed beggar
there probably lost an arm in the battle of Zama. Do you see
now that Rome, the city of justice, is full of cruel injustice?"

Another time Cornelia took the children out to the countryside, to the great estates and farms outside Rome. And on the
farms which were all owned by a few patrician families they
could see hundreds of slaves (some with leg-chains to prevent
them running away) working in the fields. Among them overse-
ers walked with whips and would lash anyone who did not work
fast enough or well enough.

When the boys saw this they said to their mother: "But it is not right that the rich patricians own all the land and work it with slaves. The poor, the soldiers who have fought for Rome, they should not live in the slums of Rome. They should each have a little plot of land that they can work themselves."

Their mother answered: "Yes, it was so once – but things have changed."

And the boys said: "Then we will change it back again, we will devote our lives to bring fairness and true justice back to Rome."

Cornelia not only saw that her boys were taught the usual things a young patrician had to learn to be clever, but that she wanted them to grow up as good men with a sense of fairness and justice.

She loved her sons dearly. One day a very rich patrician lady came in the evening for a visit. That patrician lady was very proud of the precious stones, the jewels she possessed. She was chatting with Cornelia and said: "Look at this pearl necklace I am wearing – is it not wonderful? And look at the emeralds and sapphires and diamonds in my rings – don't they sparkle and shine like stars? But what about you, my dear Cornelia, have you no precious jewels to show me?"

And Cornelia said: "Oh yes, I have. I will show them to you."

And she led the vain lady to the room where her two boys were asleep, and pointing to them said: "These are my jewels, the only ones of which I am proud." The lady felt rather ashamed and soon departed.

But when they grew up the two boys, Tiberius and Gaius Gracchus, became men of whom their mother could be proud, even though they lost their lives for the sake of fairness and justice.

# 18. The Cause of the Plebeians

There was a time long before the wars with Carthage when the plebeians walked out of Rome and said they were going to build a city of their own, but the patricians persuaded them to come back. At that time the patricians promised the plebeians that every year they could choose a patrician who would speak for the plebeians in the Senate. This man was given the title Tribune. Whenever a patrician took advantage of a poor plebeian, whenever plebeians were treated unfairly, then this Tribune would speak up for them in the Senate and the Senators would have to listen to him and would have to put things right.

It was even written into the law that the plebeians should elect a different Tribune each year who should defend their rights. The most important laws of Rome were engraved on twelve stone-tablets and this law that the plebeians should elect a Tribune every year was one of those written on the stone-tablets, it was so important.

But the Tribunes themselves were patricians, and in the course of time they did less and less for the plebeians. Full of hope every year the plebeians elected another man as Tribune, and every year they were disappointed, for the man they had chosen never spoke up for them.

The two sons of Cornelia, Tiberius and Gaius, were brought up by their mother to see the wrong that was done to the plebeians, to the men who had fought for Rome and had no thanks for it. Tiberius, the elder, was the first of the two to make it his task to do something for the plebeians.

Every educated Roman was trained to speak well in public, to be a good orator. It was again something which the Romans copied from the Greeks. Tiberius Gracchus, too, was trained to make public speeches. Tiberius went to the Forum and standing on the rostrum (from which the leaders of Rome used to speak to the people) he spoke many times to the plebeians.

"The wild beasts of the forests have their caves and dens, but the soldiers who have brought glory and treasures to Rome have no land and no house of their own. The rich patricians, who do not know how to handle a plough, own all the land and make slaves do the work, while the strong arms of brave Romans must be idle. But if you plebeians make me your spokesman, your Tribune, then I will see to it that the patricians give up some of their land and this land shall be divided among you. You shall have your own little farms again."

The plebeians came in their thousands to listen to Tiberius Gracchus and new hope grew in their hearts. And when the time came to elect a new Tribune, they chose Tiberius. Tiberius went to the Senate and he told the Senators that there was no justice, no fairness in Rome, unless land was taken from the rich and given to the plebeians.

Now the Senators were themselves rich land-owners, and had no wish to give up even the tiniest bit of land. But they were cunning men, who did not say "No" to Tiberius. They said, "Yes, you are quite right, but you must understand that it will take some time until we have worked out how much land every one of us has to give up."

And among themselves, the Senators said: "This young man, Tiberius Gracchus is a nuisance, but he can only be Tribune for one year, so it is written on the twelve stone-tablets. And if we can drag things out and move as slowly as possible with the dividing of the land, then the year will be over, and another man will be Tribune. Then it will be as it has always been, a man who will be on our side, we shall see to that."

And so when the year had passed, the Senators had done hardly anything at all to divide the land. But Tiberius spoke to the plebeians and asked them to choose him as Tribune again. And they all shouted: "Yes, we want Tiberius as Tribune." He became Tribune for the second year running. But the cunning Senators rubbed their hands with glee, for Tiberius had broken the law which said he could only be Tribune for one year.

By order of the Senators, a Consul with soldiers was sent to Tiberius. When the crowds of plebeians saw them coming, they fled, only a few staying with Tiberius. Tiberius could not put up a fight and he tried to flee to the Temple of Jupiter on the Capitoline Hill. This temple was an asylum and no one inside the temple could be taken by force or killed. But the doors of the temple were closed by patricians before he could get in. And so Tiberius was killed on the steps of the temple by the Consul and his men.

Cornelia, his mother, took the news in true Roman spirit. She did not shed any tears, but she said to Gaius, her younger son: "Now it is your turn to carry on with your brother's task."

Gaius Gracchus was an even better orator than his brother, the plebeians cheered him whenever he spoke, and he was made their Tribune. But Gaius did not let the Senators put off the division of the land, they had agreed that it was right to give land back to the plebeians and now they had to do it. Of course, the Senators and all the patricians hated Gaius even more than they had hated his brother. But they could do nothing as long as he did not break the law. And so land was given back to the old soldiers and their families – they could live as peasants again on their own little plot and in their own simple huts. But the patricians and Senators never forgave Gaius for taking land away from them, they waited for an opportunity to kill him as they had killed his brother.

Soon Gaius gave them that opportunity. He came with a new idea: he wanted to build a new city on the site where Carthage had stood. In that new city the poor of Rome could find new homes, as not all plebeians had been given land in Italy, for there was not enough for everybody.

Many Romans, patricians as well as plebeians, hated the idea of having a city where the great enemy Carthage had stood. But others were for it, and soon Rome was divided into those for and those against a new Carthage. People even fought each other in the streets, and in these street-fights one of the Lictors (the men who bore the fasces before the Consul) was killed. In the eyes of the Romans, with their great respect for law, the killing of a Lictor was a terrible crime, and the Senators blamed Gaius for it, as it had been his followers who had killed the Lictor.

Now the Senators again had an excuse to send a Consul and soldiers against a Gracchus. Gaius did not want to be executed like a criminal, so he ordered a faithful slave to kill him with a dagger. The slave obeyed, and then killed himself.

So Cornelia had lost both her sons. But she never showed any outward signs of grief. She continued to lived outside Rome in a country-house for another ten years. But later the Roman patricians were ashamed of what had been done to the two brothers. They honoured the memory of Tiberius and Gaius, and gave special honour to Cornelia. In the Forum a statue of Cornelia was put up with an inscription to say that she was a great and noble woman and the mother of two great and noble sons.

For in the end the patricians realised that until the plebeians had been treated fairly and justly, Rome would never become a great power. Rome's might was then still growing, but could not have continued if patricians and plebeians had been at war with each other. That is why, in the end, even the patricians honoured the memory of the Gracchi.

# 19. Marius

Through Tiberius and Gaius Gracchus reforms were brought that the plebeians could at least have a little plot of land of their own, and although it was not much and they were still poor at least they were master of their own land. Another change came which was that a plebeian could become an officer and a general in the Roman legions, and could even become a Consul.

One such plebeian was Marius. Marius did not grow up in Rome itself but in a village in the mountains near Rome. Being the son of poor peasants he had no education, he had no tutors to teach him philosophy and other subjects or good manners or how to make speeches. He grew up among wild, rough boys, and he was the wildest and roughest among them. He and his gang of friends would roam the mountain-side even in pouring rain, and many a time they would spend the night sleeping in the open. The other boys all admired Marius for he would scale the steepest cliffs, he would tackle wolves with his short spear, he would swim the rushing mountain streams. Of course, Marius was always the leader among these boys; if any of the boys stood up against Marius, there was a fight which always ended with Marius winning. He wanted to be a leader, he could not stand having somebody above him.

It was only natural that when Marius was old enough, he became a soldier in the Roman army. His life in the mountains had prepared him well for the hardships of a soldier's life. Long marches and fierce fighting were things that suited Marius. He made an excellent soldier and soon became an officer.

At that time Rome was at war with Numidia, a country on the north coast of Africa. The king of Numidia, Jugurtha, was an evil man: he had murdered the previous king and his son, who were friends and allies of Rome, to make himself ruler of Numidia. To revenge the murder of their ally, the previous king, the Romans sent an army to Africa under General Metellus. Marius was one of Metellus' officers.

But it was not easy to fight and to march in the blazing hot sun of Africa. The native warriors of Numidia were of course used to it, but for the Roman soldiers it was exhausting, and they made only very slow progress. But Marius' soldiers all admired their officer. He marched by their side in the glaring heat of the sun, he shared the precious water in his water bottle with his men. And when they were digging trenches, Marius himself took a spade and dug harder than anyone else.

While Marius was popular with the soldiers, he was not very popular with his general, Metellus. Metellus was a haughty patrician and had no great liking for the uncouth, rough plebeian, Marius. And Marius hated the proud patrician and felt certain that he himself would make a much better general. Marius was an ambitious man: he wanted to show that although he had grown up as a peasant boy in a tiny village, he was a better man than all these arrogant patricians.

And so Marius sent letters and messages from Africa to the Senate in Rome, telling them that Metellus was far too slow in the war against the Numidians – he, Marius, could do much better. It was not a proper thing to do, but nevertheless he did it. And then one day, he simply told Metellus: "I have had enough of this. I am going back to Rome to be elected as Consul. I will come back as a Consul and then I will be in command here, not you."

Metellus was furious, but could do nothing. And Marius did return to Rome where Senators who wanted to end the war in Africa did believe him, and made him Consul. And so the plebeian Marius came back to Africa as Consul, but Metellus returned to Rome for he was too proud to let Marius command him.

One of the hardest cities to take was a mountain-fortress, on high steep cliffs, a fortress where Jugurtha, the evil king, had hidden a large part of his treasure. Marius' troops laid siege to the fortress, but the defenders had plenty of food, and so weeks passed and the Romans could not take the fortress – it was quite impossible to storm the steep cliffs.

One day one of the soldiers stood at the foot of one of these rocks. And looking up he saw a few snails on a ledge. The Romans liked to eat snails, it was a delicacy for them. So when the soldier saw these snails he climbed up on the ledge to pick up the snails. He looked round for more snails for his friends. He found he could climb a bit higher, and still higher, and, to his own surprise, going from ledge to ledge, he reached the top of the cliff. There was a great oak tree that reached well over the wall of the fortress. And there was no guard anywhere to be seen. The defenders of the fortress, the Numidians, thought this part of the cliffs so steep and so safe that they had not thought to have any guards there. The soldier quickly climbed down and reported to Marius what he had found, and now Marius showed that he was really a clever general.

At his orders one part of his troops pretended to attack the fortress, and while the warriors of the fortress were all fighting off the Romans on one side, other soldiers silently scaled the cliff following the route their friend had discovered. Suddenly they were inside the fortress and the Numidian warriors were so startled that they threw down their arms and surrendered.

It was a splendid victory for Marius, but King Jugurtha was still free and still fought on.

# 20. The Betrayal of Jugurtha

Before continuing we shall look at the time at which these things happened. Rome had been founded by Romulus in about 750 before the birth of Christ. The wars with Carthage were only about two hundred years before Christ. And the time of Marius was only a hundred years before Christ's birth.

There was no kindness in these people of that time before Christ. The men, women and children of a conquered city were killed or sold as slaves. A human life counted for very little; there was great ambition, thirst for power, there was also courage and cunning, but no mercy. There was also a great deal of treachery, lies and deceit.

Jugurtha, the Numidian king, was still fighting on. And not only that, but another African king, Bocchus, who was his father-in-law, came to his help. So Marius now had two enemies to fight: Jugurtha and Jugurtha's father-in-law. And Marius became very worried for if he could not end the war quickly, the Senators in Rome would not be pleased. Marius wanted to remain Consul for the rest of his life. That was now his ambition. But if he failed to end the war with Jugurtha quickly, there was no chance that the Senators would make him Consul again.

But – so thought Marius – perhaps this ally of Jugurtha, his father-in-law, might be won over to the Roman side. And so Marius sent messengers to King Bocchus, saying: "Do not imagine that we Romans shall not win in the end. We shall win, no matter how long it takes, as we have won over Carthage before. And we Romans are terrible to our enemies – but we are generous to our friends. Show yourself now as a friend of Rome, and Rome will be your friend and ally and crush your enemies."

"But how can I show myself as friend of Rome?" asked the king.

"It is quite simple," answered the Romans. "Jugurtha trusts you. Deliver him into our hands, and Rome will always be your friend. But if you do not do as we tell you, then sooner or later you and Jugurtha will both end in misery."

And King Bocchus, Jugurtha's father-in-law, became so frightened of the Romans that in the end he decided to betray his son-in-law. He asked Marius to send a Roman officer and some soldiers to whom he could hand over Jugurtha.

When the Roman officer, Sulla, and his men arrived, King Bocchus sent a messenger to invite Jugurtha. The message was: "Your father-in-law has taken some Roman prisoners. Will you please come and take them."

And Jugurtha, who trusted his father-in-law, came. But as soon as he entered the tent of King Bocchus, armed guards fell on him, tied his hands and he was handed over to the Romans.

They brought Jugurtha to Marius who had him put in chains and sent to Rome. In Rome Jugurtha was led in these chains through the streets, pelted with stones by the people, and thrown into a damp, cold prison. He said with a bitter smile: "How cold your baths are, Romans." And in this wet, cold prison he soon died.

So Marius had kept his promise to the Senate, he had ended the war in Numidia, and the Senators were so grateful that he was made Consul a second time, and then a third and even a fourth time. Marius, the plebeian, had become the most powerful man in Rome.

But Sulla, the officer who took Jugurtha prisoner, was to become Marius' greatest enemy, and in time became even more powerful than Marius.

# 21. The People from the North

After the war in Africa, Marius returned to Rome where he was appointed Consul four times. There was a good reason why the Senators made the same man Consul so often: Rome was in great danger from a new, terrible enemy, and there was no better man to save Rome than this tough, ruthless soldier, Marius.

Once before an enemy had invaded Italy from the North, coming across the Alps – Hannibal and his mercenaries. This time another enemy came across the Alps into Italy. But these invaders were not people who came from hot countries; like Hannibal's troops, they were northern people and quite different, the Romans had never seen anything like these people before.

They were tall, hardly any of them were less than six feet tall. They were fair-skinned, and had flaxen hair that fell down to their shoulders, and blond beards. These tall men were dressed in animal-skins, on their helmets they wore birds' wings or animal horns, they had big shields and long swords. These wild men from the North took great pride in their strength and hardiness. When they came to the snow-covered passes of the Alps, they threw off their clothing and, laughing and shouting, they climbed naked through falling snow and over ice-covered rocks. And behind the men there came their women-folk and the children in ox-carts and horse-carts. And the women were as tall and strong and fair as the men.

So it was not just an army, but a whole nation, several tribes of these wild northerners who came across the Alps. To them, cold, ice, snow were friends and they rejoiced in them. When they had reached the top of the mountain passes the men took their broad shields, turned them into sledges and sledged down the snow-covered slopes.

Hundreds and thousands of them arrived in Italy. These tall, fair-haired barbarians of enormous strength reached a river in Northern Italy, and across the river they saw a camp of Roman legions, which had been gathered and sent North to stop the invaders.

The wild men, who had crossed the Alps as if it were a holiday outing, decided first to build a dam in the river before attacking the Romans. And the Roman soldiers – watching from their camp – were struck with awe at their strength. Great trees were uprooted and thrown into the river as if they were saplings, enormous rocks were hurled into the stream as if they were stones. It was a sight that filled the Roman soldiers' hearts with dread.

And when the barbarians prepared themselves for battle, the first lines, the front ranks of warriors were fastened together by long chains that were slipped through their belts so that a long line of men could not be broken. Just before the battle began they all lifted their shields before their mouths and they roared a wild battle-cry which the shields made even louder so that it was like thunder.

Once they began, these tall men from the North – so it seemed to the Romans – went mad, fighting with a wild fury, a rage that the Romans had never encountered before. They hit and slashed without caring whether they themselves were wounded or killed; the wounded fought on lying on the ground. Barbarians whose swords broke, fought on with bare hands and crushed Roman heads with their fists before they fell to Roman swords.

In the first battles the Roman legions fled in terror, and the cities of Northern Italy were laid waste by the invaders. The Romans called these wild people Cimbri and Teutons, and their fighting fury was called *furor Teutonicus*. The word *Deutsch* comes from "Teutons."

# 22. Rome is Saved

Imagine how terrified the people in Rome were – they were only too glad to make Marius Consul for a fifth time if only he would rid them of these wild people, the Cimbri and Teutons, from the North.

And Marius was the right man for this task, not only because he was fearless himself, but also because the soldiers knew him so well and trusted him and had confidence in him. It was a common saying among the Roman legionaries: "When Marius leads us, then victory is certain. And usually there is a nice lot of plunder, as well."

So when Marius took command of the army against the wild barbarians, his soldiers were of good heart. The first battle was against one part of the wild invaders, the Teutons. Now the Teutons were eager to fight, and would not wait for the Romans to attack them, but would attack first; Marius knew this. He let his soldiers build a fortified camp on a hill, while he himself hid with one part of his troops in a wood further down, in the plain.

Then the Teutons came. Roaring their wild battle-cry, they stormed uphill against the camp, but their wild rush was stopped. The Romans with their short swords could stab quicker than the barbarians could hit with their long heavy swords. And the wild men from the North lost heart and retreated downhill. At that moment Marius and his men came from their ambush. Now the barbarians were caught between two Roman forces, they were not used to such fighting at all, there was total confusion, and the barbarians were slaughtered. At the end of the battle the field was covered with thousands of dead Teutons.

The other invaders, the Cimbri, knew nothing of what had happened to their allies. When they saw Manus and his troops approaching, they sent messengers to say that they would spare the Romans' lives if they were given land to settle in Italy.

"Oh yes," answered Marius, "I will give you as much land as I have given your friends, the Teutons."

"How much land was that?" asked the messengers.

"For each man a hole in the ground," Marius replied, "for we killed them all."

When the messengers brought this news to the Cimbri, a great shout of rage and fury went up and they prepared to avenge the death of their friends.

But they had chosen a bad day for the battle, for it was a hot summer's day in Italy, and the summer can be unbearably hot there. However, the Roman soldiers were used to fighting in greater heat, in Africa, while the Cimbri were only good fighters in cold weather. The burning heat of the Italian summer made them feel faint and weak, and more and more of them fell to the Roman swords. Some barbarians tried to flee, but they were tied by their chains to each other; the chains got entangled and in the confusion the Romans killed them like sheep.

Some barbarians freed themselves from the chains and ran back to the carts with the women and children. But the women shouted: "Back into the fight you cowards!" and struck their own men with axes and swords.

When the Roman soldiers came the women would not surrender either, they fought as fiercely as men. In the end when they could no longer hold the Romans off, the women who were still alive killed the children and strangled themselves with their long hair rather than become slaves.

And so the barbarians from the North were defeated by Marius. But a long, long time later, five hundred years later, other wild tribes came from the North and conquered Rome and shattered the Roman empire. In the end the slaughter of the Cimbri and Teutons was avenged. But at that time Marius was praised and honoured by the Senate and people of Rome for he had saved them from the wild barbarians.

# 23. Marius: Public Enemy

When Marius had saved Rome from the Cimbri and the Teutons, the Senators were so grateful that they made him Consul for a sixth term. And Marius loved to be the most powerful man in Rome, he was proud and ambitious, and he wanted to continue being Consul.

But Marius was only a great Consul in wartime; he could lead armies into battle. In peacetime he was not a good Consul. A Consul often had to make public speeches in the Forum, or in the Senate, and Marius – who had never been trained to speak well in his youth – was a poor speaker: he was shy, he could hardly put into words what he had to say, he slurred his words. The Romans did not think much of a Consul who could not speak well.

But there was something else. There were still two parties in Rome, the patricians and the plebeians, who quarrelled with each other. Whenever there was an argument between patricians and plebeians, the Consul was supposed to make a fair and just decision. But Marius was only skilled on the battlefield, he was not skilled in these political decisions, and in any case the patricians would always say: "He is a plebeian himself, he will always favour the plebeians."

So in peacetime Marius was not a great success as a Consul. The patricians complained all the time that a man without education was not fit to be a Consul. The Senators (who were, of course, patricians themselves) had had enough of this unrefined soldier Marius, and the next year they chose as Consul the patrician, Sulla, the officer who had once taken Jugurtha prisoner.

This was a hard blow for Marius' pride. He was no longer the highest man in Rome. It was also a hard blow that he was no longer Commander of the Roman army, because the Consul was always the highest general in Rome. But what hurt Marius most was that Sulla – a much younger man who had been an officer under him – was now Commander of the Roman forces.

Marius was full of bitterness, full of hurt pride that the Romans, who had praised him no end when they were in danger from the barbarians, no longer wanted him, and had put that young patrician Sulla in his place.

Then a war broke out, a war in Africa. And, of course, Sulla, as Consul, was gathering men and getting them ready for sailing east. But Marius could not bear the thought that there should be a war and fighting, with somebody else leading the Roman legions.

Now Marius had many friends among the plebeians, and they started a rebellion in Rome. Armed plebeians filled the Forum, and the Senators, in fear of their lives, made a law that Marius should be commander of the Roman army.

The rioting plebeians had looked everywhere for Sulla in order to kill him. But he escaped from Rome and reached the camp on the coast where his soldiers were gathering for the war in Africa. Sulla spoke to his soldiers, and told them how Marius had broken the law and had himself appointed commander by force.

"Do you want a law-breaker as your leader?" he shouted.

"No" answered the soldiers, "we will follow you Sulla, the rightful Consul of Rome."

And Sulla now marched his army into Rome. The plebeians knew they would be no match against trained soldiers, they did not even try to fight. The Senators were only too pleased that Sulla had come to their rescue. And now they passed a law declaring Marius and his supporters who had stirred up the rebellion to be public enemies, which meant that every Roman citizen had not only the right, but the duty to kill them.

Marius' friends were caught and killed, but he escaped. And now Marius – the man who had once saved Rome, the man who for six years had been the most powerful man in Rome – was a homeless fugitive, who could be killed by any Roman citizen.

# 24. Marius in Exile

What was it that had brought Marius to such a state that his life was no longer safe, that he was a homeless man, a fugitive? It was his pride and ambition. It had been pride and ambition which had ruled him when he made himself leader of the boys in his native village. It had been pride and ambition which made him quarrel with his general in Africa, until he himself became Consul and army leader. It was pride and ambition that made him want to remain Consul, year after year. And now it was through pride and ambition that he had lost everything.

Now he paid a heavy price for his pride. He reached the coast and saw a ship. He had brought money with him and he offered the sailors a rich reward if they would take him away from Italy. The sailors agreed, but as soon as they were at sea, they changed their mind. Why should they risk punishment, perhaps death, for the sake of Marius? So they sailed back and put him ashore, saying: "We have not killed you, as would have been our duty, we won't even hand you over to the soldiers who are searching everywhere for you, but we will not have anything to do with you."

Marius was left to himself. He found the hut of an old peasant who gave him shelter. But he had only rested for a few hours in the old man's hut when he heard the clatter of horses' hooves of a search-party of soldiers. In despair Marius rushed from the hut and reached a marshy field. Finding a wet, muddy ditch, he hid himself there. But the horsemen dismounted and searched every yard for him. At last they found Marius and dragged him out, covered with mud.

He was marched to prison in the nearest town, a sad figure, covered with dirt and mud. The soldiers could have killed Marius straightaway, but they could not bring themselves to kill the man who a few years before had been their leader. They

would rather hand him over to the nearest judge who would
have the job of executing Marius.

The judge of the little town where Marius was held in prison
soon found that it was not easy to execute Marius, for no one,
no citizen and no soldier was willing to go in and kill him. They
all refused. At last the judge found a slave who was not a Roman,
but a Gaul, who was willing for a reward to go into the prison
and kill Marius.

The slave went into the dark prison, sword in hand. At first
he could see nothing in the darkness, and then he saw two fierce
eyes looking at him, and the slave began to shake with fear. And
then a mighty voice roared at him: "Fellow, dare you kill the
great Marius?"

The slave turned and rushed out, crying: "I cannot kill him!"

The judge and the citizens decided they did not want to have
anything to do with the terrible Marius. They took him from
the prison and put him on a boat that sailed to Africa. So Marius
had escaped certain death because people could not forget how
much he had done for Rome.

But even in Africa he was never safe, for ever fleeing from
one place to another. Whoever gave him shelter would not allow
him to stay long. It was a hard time for Marius and, in his heart,
he swore he would revenge himself one day on his enemies in
Rome, on Sulla and the patricians, who had brought him so low.

But in the meantime, things in Rome changed and brought
the time nearer when Marius could revenge himself.

# 25. Marius' Return

Marius had gone through hard times, but hard times did not make him humble, and although he was by then already an old man of almost seventy, he was still as proud and as ambitious as ever. And he was also revengeful. It did not occur to him that he had broken the law, that he was in the wrong, that his own pride had brought his downfall. No, all he thought of was that his enemies, Sulla, and many of the patricians had brought him down.

And, in his mind he recalled every man, every patrician who had ever spoken against him, who had ever made remarks about his poor speeches, and he promised himself that, when the time came, every one of them would pay with his life for daring to speak against Marius.

But while Marius was dreaming of revenge in Africa, there were great changes in Rome. Once Marius had been driven out, Sulla, Consul and Commander of the Roman army, sailed with his army to Asia. But that war in Asia lasted a long time, and so Sulla was away from Rome for a long time.

The Senators decided that while Sulla was away, Rome needed two Consuls to keep order in the city. They chose a plebeian, Cinna, and a patrician, Octavius.

But it was not a wise decision. There was soon quarrels and hatred between the two Consuls, and instead of keeping order the two Consuls made Rome a place of disorder and fighting between the two parties.

Cinna wanted to alow Marius to return to Rome. The Senators did not like the idea at all, but Cinna said: "Let the people of Rome themselves decide if they want Marius back. Let them all come to the Forum and vote for or against Marius' return." And the Senators had to agree to this.

But when the people of Rome were assembled in the Forum

to give their vote, Cinna led a band of armed men into the Forum and it was quite clear that these armed men would strike down anybody who would vote against Marius' return.

Of course, that was against all law and against all justice. The other Consul, the patrician Octavius, could not let this happen, and he came with armed men to drive Cinna and his followers away.

Fierce fighting broke out on the Forum. Unarmed citizens fled in terror while the armed men on either side fought a battle right in front of the Senate and the great temples of the Forum. In the end, most of Cinna's men were killed, though Cinna himself escaped. Then the Senators declared that Cinna had broken the law, that he could no longer be Consul, and that he was a public enemy.

But Cinna was furious that his plan had not come off. He was not going to flee, but was going to gather an army to fight Octavius. Not only that, but he was going to get Marius to join him. Together they would enter Rome, kill their enemies and make themselves masters of Rome. This was Cinna's plan. And while he gathered an army from among the plebeians, his messengers found Marius in Africa and, old though he was, Marius returned with them to Italy for he was still filled with pride, ambition and lust for revenge.

# 26. The Death of Marius

It was very clever of Cinna, the plebeian Consul, to have called Marius to his side. For the name of Marius still worked like magic with people: thousands of men came and offered themselves as soldiers to fight under the great general who had never lost a battle. And when Octavius, the patrician Consul, marched his soldiers against his enemy, Cinna and Marius, many of his soldiers deserted him and went over to the other side. And even those of his men who stayed with Octavius were simply too frightened to fight against Marius. The only man who could have protected Rome against Marius would have been Sulla. But he and his army were still in the East, fighting a war in Asia and Greece. They could not come to the help of Rome.

The Senators were now in despair, they knew that Marius and Cinna had enough soldiers to surround Rome and starve the people until they surrendered. They agreed to surrender without a fight and hope Marius and Cinna would show themselves merciful. But they were mistaken, mercy was not a word that meant anything to Marius. He only remembered the shameful days when he had fled for his life, when he was dragged, covered with mud through the streets, and a miserable foreign slave had been sent to execute him. And when Marius thought of these days his heart became as hard as a stone and he wanted only one thing: revenge.

When Rome opened its gates, Marius and Cinna marched in at the head of their troops and reached the Forum. There they were welcomed by the Senators. But they only looked grimly at the old men, and told them what they wanted.

First, the law which made Marius and Cinna public enemies had to be abolished. The Senators agreed, and abolished the law. Next, the patrician Octavius should cease to be Consul. Again the Senators agreed, and declared that Octavius was no longer

Consul. Thirdly they demanded that Marius and Cinna should be appointed Consuls. Again the Senators agreed – they could do nothing else. And so Marius became Consul for the seventh time.

It was the task of the Consuls to uphold law and justice in Rome. But Marius and Cinna did not use their power for law and justice, they used it for mean and cruel revenge. Marius had brought with him a special bodyguard, men who knew no pity and no mercy, and he used this bodyguard to revenge himself The first patrician to be killed was Octavius, and then hundreds of others were killed. The citizens of Rome lived in fear and trembling – they prayed to the gods to rescue them from the terror of Marius.

And they were rescued. All these events had been very exciting for Marius, from a homeless fugitive he had once again risen to the highest power in Rome, he had taken a terrible vengeance on his enemies but all this excitement was too much for the heart of an old man. He collapsed suddenly and died within a few hours.

That was the end of the man who had started life as a poor peasant boy and had risen to be Consul seven times. But, as we have seen there was little happiness in his life though much bloodshed and cruelty. And when he died the Romans cursed his name.

His friend Cinna was sole Consul, and was preparing to fight Sulla who had at last finished the war in the East and was returning to Rome. But it never came to a fight, for Cinna was not popular with his soldiers as Marius had been. They had no wish to fight for him and rebelled against Cinna killing him. So when Sulla returned there was no resistance and, having a strong and loyal army, he could make himself unchallenged master of Rome.

# 27. Spartacus

The Romans of that time, whether patrician or plebeian, were like Marius, brave, courageous, resourceful, but without kindness or mercy, and they loved power above all things.

Sulla too, was like that. The first thing he did after his return was to have all men executed who had been friends of Marius or Cinna; once again hundreds paid with their life. But Sulla also wanted to ensure that he would remain Consul for as long as he liked. So he forced the Senators to make him Dictator, which meant that he was absolute master of Rome, not just for a year, but for as long as he liked – for the rest of his life.

The Roman citizens did not like it, but the executions had frightened everybody and it was safer to put up with Sulla than to speak against him. And the Roman people themselves were such a cruel lot that they hardly deserved anything better than a dictator like Sulla.

How cruel they were can be seen from the public amusement that became very popular at that time. From every war the Romans brought back many prisoners who were sold as slaves. But many of these prisoners were strong men, well trained in the use of weapons. And the Romans thought it would be a great sport to make such prisoners fight each other. The prisoner who won would be well treated and well fed until the next fight. Such fighters were called gladiators, and watching the gladiator fights became the most popular entertainment in Rome.

Big circuses were built, circles of tiers for thousands of spectators and in the great sand-covered centre these unfortunate men had to fight each other to the death. Sometimes there were only two men fighting each other, sometimes whole groups, a hundred or more, had to perform a battle. And the Romans went to these gladiator shows as people in our time go to the cinema, or to a football match. That men were killed there did not worry them at all.

However, while Sulla was dictator, something happened which the Romans had never expected. In the town of Capua (where Hannibal had once spent the winter) there was to be a big gladiator show in the circus. About two hundred prisoners had been brought together. Among these prisoners was a Greek whose name was Spartacus. And he said to the others: "Are we not fools to fight and kill each other instead of fighting our cruel Roman masters? If you follow me we shall perhaps also die, but at least we shall die fighting for our freedom – and not for the amusement of the Romans."

His fellow-prisoners all agreed. When the Roman guards came they followed them quite obediently to the circus. Before the games there was a special treat for the spectators at the circus. A whole ox had been roasted and was brought on a trolley into the circus; and stuck into the ox were hundreds of long sharp knives so that every spectator could cut a slice for himself.

But the Romans did not enjoy their slice of beef this time. At a sign from Spartacus the gladiators rushed to the trolley, drew out the long sharp knives, and struck down the guards who were completely taken by surprise. The spectators jumped up from their seats and ran for their lives. But the gladiators took proper weapons from the guards. They went into the city and called on all slaves to join them, and soon there were thousands of them. They captured an armoury where the Romans kept their weapons, and Spartacus found himself in command of a great, well-armed army with more and more slaves leaving their Roman masters.

Now all would have been well if the gladiators and slaves had listened to Spartacus – he wanted to march his army across the Alps out of Italy where each man could have made his way to his own homeland. But the gladiators did not want to do that, they wanted to rob and plunder Roman cities, and make themselves rich before leaving Italy. Spartacus, against his own wishes, stayed with them, for he would not desert his friends. But for the Romans a rebellion of gladiators and slaves was something terrible – how could one live without slaves?

One of Sulla's best generals, Pompey, was sent with a great army against the rebellious gladiators and slaves. They fought bravely, but only the gladiators had been trained to fight, while most of them were slaves who were not well trained, and so the Romans won the battle. Spartacus died fighting to his last breath. Many thousands of the slaves were taken prisoner – but a slave who had used arms against his masters could only be punished by death. But death by the sword was too honourable for a slave, for whom there was the most shameful death the Romans could think of: they were nailed to crosses. And so, only about a hundred years before Jesus died on a cross, thousands of poor slaves died in the same way.

# Caesars and Christians

# 28. Julius Caesar

In ancient India the five sons of Pandu, Yudishtira and his brothers, after a hard struggle regained their kingdom, but they really cared so little for earthly power, that they gave it all up and went as poor pilgrims to seek the gate of heaven high up in the Himalayan mountains. That was many thousands of years ago, in ancient India.

But when we come to Roman times, things had changed; now human beings loved power here on earth. At the very beginning of Rome, when Romulus began to build the walls of the new city, he did not want to share the kingship with his twin brother, Remus. He saw to it that he alone was chosen king of Rome, and when Remus mocked the low walls they had started to build, Romulus killed his own twin brother.

From the very beginning of Roman history there was a craving for power. Rome, the city of the seven hills, wanted power over other nations. Rome conquered Italy, Carthage and Greece. But among the Romans themselves there was a struggle for power, who would be master of mighty Rome?

We heard of Marius, the rough, uneducated plebeian soldier, who made the Senators elect him Consul seven times. And the Consul was the mightiest man in Rome. When Marius died, his enemy Sulla, the general who had conquered Greece, became master of Rome. When Sulla was not satisfied with being Consul, he forced the Senators to appoint him Dictator.

Now one could ask: why did Sulla bother about the Senators at all? Surely, with all the soldiers on his side he could have made himself master of Rome without taking any notice of the old Senators. But Romans were all very keen on *laws,* everything had to be done according to the law. The law was that only the Senators could appoint a dictator, and Sulla, being a Roman, wanted to be master of Rome by law. That was truly Roman –

you could do anything you liked (if you were powerful) but you had to make sure that it was all in accordance with the ancient laws.

So Sulla became Dictator, which meant among other things, that he had power over life and death of every Roman. He could order the execution of any person, and it would be done without question. And Sulla made use of this power, anyone who was careless enough to say openly that he did not like the dictator or was in the slightest way disobedient, was executed.

At that time a young man, a patrician of a noble family (descendants of Romulus, the first king of Rome) lived in Rome. This noble young patrician, fell in love with a girl who had only one fault – she was a plebeian. And the Dictator, Sulla (who was himself a proud patrician) did now allow marriage between patricians and plebeians. But the young man loved the girl and just went and married her. Sulla was furious, he had the young patrician brought before him and said: "I give you time until tomorrow to divorce that plebeian woman. If you don't, you will die."

This patrician was not only in love with his young wife, he was also very proud, and it hurt his pride that he should give in to a threat. So when Sulla let him go to arrange the divorce, he fled with his wife to the wild Sabine hills (part of the Apennines) where Sulla's soldiers could not find him.

Sulla was very angry that there was somebody who dared to disobey him, but his soldiers could not find the young patrician. The relatives of the young man, Senators and patricians, then pleaded with Sulla who in the end relented and forgave this young man.

The young patrician who had dared to disobey the mighty dictator Sulla was later on to become the most famous of all Romans – the greatest man in Roman history. His name was Gaius Julius Caesar.

As Sulla had forgiven him, Julius Caesar could return to Rome, but he felt that Sulla might change his mind and punish him. It would be wiser to keep away from Rome and Sulla. So Julius Caesar decided to travel by sea to Greece and stay there for a time, leaving his wife in Rome.

At that time the Mediterranean Sea was not at all safe for travellers; there were pirates about, who raided vessels, taking any rich passengers they found as prisoners, and only letting them go when a great sum of money had been paid to them as ransom.

Bad luck would have it that the ship on which Julius Caesar sailed was held up by such pirates. They came aboard and could easily see that this young man, in a fine toga and attended by ten of his own slaves, was just the kind of prisoner they wanted.

Julius Caesar had to go on board the pirate ship; they allowed him to keep two of his slaves, while the others were told to sail back to Rome, collect the ransom money from Caesar's family and relatives and to bring it within four weeks to a little Greek island where the pirates would be waiting. If the money was there, Caesar would be set free, if not, they would kill him.

Julius Caesar listened to all this, then he said: "How much ransom money do you want for me?"

The captain of the pirates said: "You should be worth twenty talents."

"What," shouted Julius Caesar, "twenty talents for a man like me, for a member of a family that goes right back to Romulus? I am worth at least fifty talents."

"Very well," said the surprised pirate, "then we want fifty talents."

"But let me tell you something else," said Caesar. "You ruffians are not going to enjoy the ransom money for long, for as soon as I am free I will get a crew and a ship and come after you and I will put every one of you robbers to the sword."

The pirate captain looked at this elegant young Roman and laughed loudly and said: "You are welcome to try it, but let us have the money first,"

The pirates took Caesar to the little island in the Mediterranean that was their hideout and headquarters and kept him prisoner. During his captivity Caesar did everything possible to annoy his captors. When they practised with their weapons he told them that they were clumsy louts; the pirates still only laughed at him.

To pass the time Julius Caesar made up poems, very long

poems, and he simply ordered the pirates to sit down and to listen to his poems. At first the pirates did listen to him reciting his poems, for the fun of it. But they soon got bored, they were not interested in poetry, they would rather play a game of dice or drink. And they told him so. But now Caesar became angry. And he said: "You scum, you don't like my poems? I had a mind to spare your miserable lives when I catch you, but after this insult, you will be killed, every one of you."

That a man who wrote poems should threaten them, seemed very funny to the pirates, they laughed heartily. But, a few weeks later, the slaves arrived with the fifty talents ransom money – and the pirates let Caesar go, still laughing about his threats.

Julius Caesar did not go far. He reached the next Greek island. There he called the men of the island together – promised them they could have the ransom money if they helped him against the pirates and soon he had a crew and a ship. Under his command they sailed to the island where he had been prisoner, the pirates were still celebrating the rich haul they had made, drinking and feasting. They were taken by surprise and, as Caesar had vowed, they were all killed and all their possessions were divided between the men who had fought for him.

# 29. Power

In ancient India men did not crave for power. When the Indians thought of their gods, they loved and worshipped the wisdom of the gods: that the gods were also powerful did not mean so much to the people of ancient India. And the holy men of ancient India tried to become wise, the wiser a man was, the nearer he was to the gods.

Later, in ancient Persia, Ahura Mazda was the god of goodness and truth, and Zarathustra, the great Persian holy man, taught his people that to be good and truthful brought a person nearer to the god of the shining sunlight, to Ahura Mazda. The Indians thought wisdom makes human beings more godlike, the Persians thought to be good and truthful made them more like Ahura Mazda.

But in Roman times people no longer had a feeling for the wisdom in the world, they had no longer a feeling for all that is good in the world, and they only thought of their gods as powerful beings. And the more power a man could get for himself, the more he was like a god. This is why the Romans had this craving for power; they had no feeling for wisdom, no feeling for goodness, but they felt: the more power I have, the more I am like a god.

Sulla, the cruel dictator, enjoyed being the most powerful man in the Roman Empire that had already swallowed Italy, Spain, Greece, and a part of North Africa. He enjoyed the feeling that people feared him and trembled before him. But as he grew older, he found the task of ruling this far-flung realm too hard. And so, as an old man, he gave up the dictatorship, and spent his last years as a private citizen in great luxury and comfort.

The people of Rome sighed with relief when Sulla retired from the dictatorship, and everybody in Rome, patricians and plebeians, Senators and soldiers, had only one wish: not to have another dictator, not to walk again in fear of one's life.

But now that Sulla had gone, there were also some who wanted the power which Sulla had wielded: but they realised that after the terrible years of Sulla's dictatorship, it would not be so easy to get this power. Not only the Senators, but the whole population of Rome would resist if anybody tried to take Sulla's place.

One man who was ambitious, who wanted power for himself, was Julius Caesar. One day with some friends he rode through a tiny village of poor peasants. "What a poor, wretched little place," said one of his friends.

"Yes, it is," said Julius Caesar, "but I would sooner be the first man in this village, than the second man in great Rome."

But Julius Caesar was careful not to show his ambitions, his dreams of power, to the people of Rome. On the contrary, he pretended that all he cared for was an easy life of pleasure. He dressed in the most exquisite togas, he had a barber to trim his hair every day – and so everyone in Rome thought that a man who cared so much about his hair could not care for serious things such as power. He was also clever in making himself popular with the common people of Rome. One of the main streets of Rome, the Appian Way, was in very bad condition, muddy in rain, ankle-deep dust in the summer. He had it repaired and paved at his own expense. Sometimes he invited the people of Rome to a free evening in the Arena, he paid for all the seats – and the citizens could watch chariot-races and gladiators without having to pay for it. They liked that very much, and they liked Julius Caesar who was so generous to give them free entertainment. (In later times all Roman rulers continued this custom – it was an easy way to gain the affection of the people.)

When Julius Caesar had made himself popular in this way, he took another step towards his goal of power: he made a secret agreement with two important Romans. One was the very successful general, Pompey (the town of Pompeii was named in his honour), and the other was the richest man in Rome, Crassus.

And what Caesar said to Pompey and Crassus was this: "I am now so popular with the people of Rome, with the common people, that they cheer whenever they see me. If I asked them to vote for me, they would do it. But I am afraid the Senators don't like me, they don't trust me, the only way to get round the Senators is to bribe them, to make large gifts of money to them. I am not rich enough for that – but you Crassus, you could do it, you are very rich. So with money we could get the Senators on our side. And if there are still any people against us, your soldiers love you, Pompey, and will fight for you whenever you give the order. So the three of us together can get to power in Rome: we shall share the power."

And Pompey and Crassus agreed, for they too had the Roman craving for power. But they kept their pact a secret, waiting for the right time to make themselves masters of Rome.

So Sulla had retired, but there were other men, cunning and clever, who wanted to take his place.

# 30. Gaul

In Roman times, the wisdom of India and the goodness of ancient Persia had gone, and all there was, specially in Rome, was a feeling that the gods were powerful, and the more powerful a man was, the more he was like a god.

But there was one country, a very small country, which was different: the land of the people whom Moses had thousands of years earlier led out of Egypt, the "promised" land, the land of Palestine.

Among the people of that land, the Jews, there was the law of Moses, which said (like the religion of Zarathustra) that God wants human beings to be good, that before God goodness alone counts, not power.

All the surrounding nations – Egypt, Rome, even Greece – worshipped their gods because a god must be a powerful being. The Jews called God all-powerful, but they also called him a God of Mercy, they worshipped his goodness, much more than his power.

The Roman general Pompey who, together with the rich man Crassus, made a secret pact with Julius Caesar, also craved for power. He had found another way of becoming popular with the people of Rome: he did not give them free entertainment as Julius Caesar did, but he conquered more countries for Rome. The Romans liked a general who had great victories, who spread the power of Rome wider and wider.

Among other countries Pompey also conquered Palestine, the land of the Israelites, for Rome. The Jews fought bravely for their homeland, but they were no match for the might of the Roman armies. And so Pompey brought the Holy Land, Palestine, under Roman power, and Roman soldiers marched through the streets of Jerusalem, the Holy City.

Other nations that had been conquered by the Romans in time accepted Roman rule, they copied Roman manners and Roman customs, they even worshipped the Roman gods. But not the Jews. The Jews always hated the Roman masters, they did not imitate Roman customs – and they worshipped only the one God who had given the ten commandments to Moses.

But whether the people of Palestine liked it or not, did not matter to the Romans. They were proud that another country had been added to their conquests, and they praised Pompey and called him Pompey the Great.

Even though Julius Caesar had a secret pact with Crassus and with Pompey, there was no real friendship between the three men. And Caesar was not at all happy to hear Pompey praised for his conquests. He had to show the Romans that he too could make conquests, that he was a general as good or even better than Pompey. And so Caesar asked the Senators to give him command of an army for the conquest of a great country northwest of Italy, the great country of Gaul, the country which is now called France.

The Senators thought it was a good idea to get such a dangerous man as Julius Caesar away from Rome. As long as he was marching and fighting far away from Rome he could not cause any trouble in Rome. So Julius Caesar was given an army and marched north to conquer Gaul.

The people who had only known Caesar as a man who lived in comfort and luxury in Rome would have been very surprised if they had seen him with his army. When his soldiers marched, he did not ride on his horse, but walked beside them (and it was long, fast marching in the Roman army), he ate no other food than the common soldiers, and in any battle you could find Caesar where the fighting was hardest.

Once in a rainstorm Caesar was taking shelter in a little hut on the roadside, when he saw a wounded man carried by his comrades on a stretcher. Caesar immediately gave orders that the wounded man should be put into the hut, and as there was not enough room he himself slept outside in the rain with his soldiers.

These kind of things made Caesar very popular with the

common soldiers, they loved the general who shared their dangers and their discomfort. But the officers did not like it at all. They did not like to march when they had horses to ride, they did not like the plain food of the common soldier, but they had to do as Caesar did, and they grumbled.

And the grumbling got worse and worse until, one day Caesar gave the order that all his troops, his whole army should assemble, should be on parade. When they were all standing in ranks before him, each legion with their own officers, he spoke to the grumbling officers and said that spoilt weaklings were no use to him and that any officer or common soldier who was afraid of long marches and hard fighting had his permission to creep back to Rome. "But," so said Caesar, "I will keep one legion with me, the Tenth Legion, for the soldiers of the Tenth Legion are real men."

The whole Tenth Legion cheered loudly when they heard this, and all the grumbling officers were so ashamed that they went to Caesar and begged to be allowed to stay with him. From that day onwards Caesar had no more complaints, all his soldiers were proud to serve under him.

# 31. The Celtic People

The large country which we now call France, and which in Caesar's time was called Gaul, was quite different from what it is now. There were no fields of golden wheat, no vineyards, there was no "garden" south of the Loire and no great cities. Most of the land was covered with vast forests, larger and darker than any you have seen, and in these forests prowled wolves, bears, and wild boars.

And the people who lived in these forests were also fierce and proud. These people of Gaul were tall with blue eyes and fair or red hair. Their dress was simple: the men wore short tunics, round their feet they wrapped cloth held together by leather thongs, and slung over their shoulders they wore a kind of cloak. The language they spoke was a kind of Gaelic – the word Gaelic means the language of Gaul. These people of the great forests of Gaul belong to the same great family of peoples to which the Scottish Highlanders, the Irish and the Welsh belong. Together they are called Celtic peoples, or Celts.

At that time all the countries we now call France, Britain, Ireland – in fact the whole of western Europe – was inhabited by Celtic peoples, but they were never united as one nation, they lived in separate tribes and clans who were often at war fighting each other.

Just as the Jews in Palestine had the feeling as in ancient Persia that God wants human beings to be good, so the Celtic people had retained something that had once existed in ancient India. They had a feeling for the wisdom of the world. When the sun rose in the sky they not only saw light filling the world, but for these Celtic people it was as if they met an infinitely wise being. Imagine meeting someone who, you feel, knows a great deal more than you can understand; in a much stronger way that was what the Celtic people felt when the sun shone upon the earth. But also winds blowing, waves splashing, all that was like a wonderful language to them. And in the soft light of the moon they saw elves and fairy-like beings working on flowers and plants and trees.

And the holy men, the priests who best understood the wisdom of the sun, the secret language of wind and waves, the elves working in plants, they were called Druids. It took a long lifetime to become worthy of being a Druid. They were old, long-bearded men, dressed in white garments. They were not only priests, but doctors, and judges in any argument, and if any man needed advice he went to the Druid. They built no closed temples, but simple circles of stones (like Stonehenge) open to the blue sky, out in nature.

Outwardly, these Celtic people may have looked wild and rough and fierce. Their dwellings were simple huts, huddled together and enclosed by an earth-wall: they built no cities and no roads. But in these rough-living people there was a great love for poetry, for song. And the men who could make poems, were called bards and were greatly respected. They had no writing: all poems were sung by heart, and all the knowledge and wisdom of the Druids was learned by heart.

Outwardly they were a rough, fierce people, but their hearts were open to the wisdom and beauty of Nature. Like the wise men of India, the priests of Gaul, of the Celtic people, knew that when people die, their soul returns to earth and is born again.

Now the Celtic people of Gaul had for some time been plagued by invasions and raids by Germanic tribes from Germany. And they had asked the Romans to come and help them fight these invaders. The Roman army which Caesar led across the Alps into Gaul was supposed to come to the aid of the Gauls. At first Caesar fought the German invaders. He defeated them in terrible battles, and only a few of them escaped across the River Rhine that was the border between Gaul and Germany.

But, having dealt with the Germanic invaders Caesar now

turned against the Gauls themselves. The Gauls were not one nation, but were divided into many independent tribes, and lacking the will and foresight to unite against Caesar, one tribe after another was defeated.

Yet each of these tribes fought desperately and bravely for their freedom, specially one tribe, the Nervii, who waited in ambush in a thick forest on one side of a river. The Romans arrived on the other side of that river and, having no idea that the enemy was so near, Caesar ordered his troops to prepare a camp. Some soldiers put up tents, others began to dig a trench and earth-wall to protect the camp, others went to collect wood for camp fires, and while almost every Roman soldier was busy getting the camp ready, the Nervii silently forded the river and suddenly, yelling their war-cries, came upon the Romans.

There was wild confusion: Soldiers carrying wood or having only a spade to defend themselves were cut down by the Gauls, others rushed about to get their weapons and ran into each other. It looked like complete disaster. But in all that confusion Caesar remained perfectly calm. He gave orders to sound the bugle to recall all men who had gone further away from camp, he put on his armour and with only a small number of men ready he led them to attack the Gauls.

The Tenth Legion, his favourite, who were on a hill further away, saw the fighting and dashed to his help. The Romans with their strict discipline and long training, rallied, closed their ranks and held the Gauls at bay. But one thing the Romans could not do: they could not force the Gauls to turn and flee, for the Gauls would not turn their backs on any enemy. And so the Romans killed them all, about sixty thousand.

Caesar had through his calmness and presence of mind turned what seemed a disaster into one of his greatest victories. He sent a report of this victory to Rome; it was the shortest report ever written, consisting of only three words: *Veni, vidi, vici* – I came, I saw, I conquered.

The Senators were so pleased about this victory that they ordered fifteen days celebration in Rome. There were feasts and games, day after day for two weeks, and Caesar's name was praised by everybody. The land of Gaul became part of the Roman Empire, without anyone in Rome giving a thought to the thousands of dead Nervii.

# 32. Britain

Julius Caesar was a clever man. He knew that once an enemy was defeated, the best option was to be generous, then in time the enemy might become friendly. Many of the tribes who fought against him found that when they surrendered, he did not execute their chiefs, he took no men or women to be sold as slaves, he only demanded that they recognise the rule of Rome. It was something rare to be so merciful in those days, but it was a very clever policy of Caesar.

To one kind of people in Gaul he showed no mercy. Yet they were people who had never fought him at all, for they were not allowed to take part in any fighting; they were the Druids. Caesar had no mercy for the Druids and they were killed by the Romans wherever they found them, and perhaps because they were the leaders, people would always listen to them. Once these leaders were gone, there was little chance of a rebellion against Rome. Without Druids the Gauls would soon take up Roman religion and Roman customs, and forget that they were Celts. So this was not just cruelty, it was a well-considered plan by Caesar.

While he was in Gaul, Caesar often heard of an island lying only a short distance across the sea north of Gaul, an island called Britain. He also heard that there in Britain Anglesey was was the most holy centre of the Druids where every Druid had been once. It was also reported that some tribes of that island of Britain had sent help to their friends in Gaul when they fought against the Romans.

Caesar thought that it might be a good thing to cross over to this island and teach the tribes there a lesson. And perhaps it would be worthwhile to make another great conquest. There was only one difficulty: to get from Gaul to Britain one needed ships, and Caesar had no ships. But this was really only a minor difficulty, for a Roman soldier was not only a well trained fighter, but he was also an expert builder. Their walls and fortresses and roads still stand today: they were all built by legionaries. And these legionaries of Rome were also trained to be carpenters and ship-builders, so when Caesar needed ships, he had the men to make them and all the forests of Gaul to give him the wood.

And so the day came when about eighty Roman ships carrying twelve thousand men led by Julius Caesar, approached the coast of Britain near Deal. The Britons who had heard rumours of Caesar's coming and seen the fleet of ships approaching, stood ready at the coast, eager to fight off the invaders.

But the Romans found to their dismay that their ships could not reach the shore – the sea was too shallow and if the ships had gone further they would have got stuck in the sand. Undismayed, Caesar gave the order: "Jump into the sea and wade ashore!"

But, brave as the Roman soldiers were, they had no heart to jump overboard into the grey, cold water. Even the brave Tenth Legion stood as if they had not heard the general's order. But the standard bearer was not to be shamed – and with the legion's eagle-standard in hand he jumped into the water and cried: "Here goes the eagle, who will let it fall into enemy hands?"

The legionaries shouted: "There goes the honour of our legion," and they hastily leapt into the sea and followed him.

There was a fierce battle, but the Roman sword won against British battle-axes, and the Britons were driven to flight. However, Caesar found the land wild and without treasures, and soon left again. It was to be a hundred years until the Romans came again to Britain, but Caesar was the first.

# 33. The Rubicon

Rome was founded by Romulus in 752 BC. Caesar was born 652 years later in 100 BC, only a hundred years before the coming of Christ. Caesar's visit to Britain was in 54 BC.

But this first Roman invasion was only brief as Caesar did not think it worth marching further into Britain. Moreover, the country he had already conquered, Gaul, was by no means settling down peacefully under the Roman rule. Under the leadership of a young nobleman, Vercingetorix, a rebellion against the Roman masters broke out. For a time it seemed as if the Gauls who fought desperately for their freedom, would defeat the Romans by the sheer weight of their numbers.

The Gauls fought fiercely but without plan, while the Roman soldiers were trained to use their heads. The different regiments each knew in a battle what the others were doing. And their leader, Caesar, was a general who planned his battles, who had thought out every move and counter-move like a game of chess. And so in spite of the fighting fury of the Gauls, and in spite of their great number, they were defeated by the fighting skill of the Roman soldiers and by Caesar's genius and forethought as a general. The rebellion of the Gauls was crushed; Vercingetorix, their leader, was sent to Rome in chains where he languished in prison, awaiting Caesar's return to Rome where he would celebrate his triumph.

Whenever a Roman general had either won a great battle or conquered a new country he was on his return to Rome honoured by a "triumph" – a great procession to celebrate the victory. Sometimes special arches, called triumphal arches were built, through which the whole procession marched. Some of these triumphal arches still stand and can be seen in Rome to this day.

The citizens of Rome lined the streets which were garlanded with flowers. And then the procession came down the street. First, in their white togas, came the highest officials of the city of Rome (for every victory was a victory for mighty Rome), then came the soldiers, the legionaries, marching proudly in step, their armour and weapons glittering in the sun, and carrying the spoils of war, the treasures, standards and arms taken from the conquered people. It was the proudest day for a Roman soldier when he could march through the cheering crowds of Rome.

After the soldiers came a golden chariot drawn by white horses. In the chariot was the victorious general, carrying on his head a crown made of laurel leaves. Now the cheering was loudest: it was like one mighty roar. But in the chariot was a slave – and what did this slave had to do? While all that cheering went on, he had to whisper to the general: "Do not forget that you are mortal, remember that you too must die one day like any other human being." Even in this great hour, the great man should be reminded that he was only a man who would die like all men.

After the chariot with the victorious general came the sad procession of all the prisoners he had taken, who walked in chains. The Roman crowds showed no pity for the plight of the prisoners: they jeered, shouted insults at them, and laughed about their foreign clothes.

When the procession was over, the prisoners were sold as slaves. But the leaders of the conquered people, like the young Vercingetorix, were executed after the procession.

Caesar was entitled to this great honour – he was entitled to a great "triumph" in the streets of Rome – but it was a long time before he could ride in the golden chariot drawn by white horses and hear the cheers of the crowd and the whisper of the slave.

First, after having crushed the rebellion of the Gauls, he had to make sure that there would be no more uprisings against Rome. His legionaries built roads so that troops could be marched easily to every part of Gaul. Some Roman roads can still be seen today. To build these roads, first a deep ditch was dug, and a layer of hard little flint-stones was put down. Then came a layer of gravel, followed by a layer of chalk, and then gravel again. Finally a layer of stone finished the surface which was smooth and remained dry. The roads which were built in this way lasted for centuries. They were built as straight as the flight of an arrow – there were no corners and bends – because it was quickest to march soldiers by the most direct route.

As well as roads Caesar had Roman temples built after the rebellion in Gaul. This was so that when the Druids had all been killed, the Gauls should turn to Roman gods. Young noblemen of Gaul were given Roman teachers or sent to Rome to be brought up in Roman ways and Roman customs. Roman laws were introduced, and so, in time, the people of Gaul were made Romans and even became Roman soldiers. They even forgot their own language and spoke Latin, from which modern French comes.

Caesar was kept very busy in Gaul even after the rebellion had been crushed. But in the meantime there were great changes in Rome. One of the two men who had that secret pact with Caesar, Crassus, the rich man, had been killed in a battle in the East. With Crassus dead and Caesar away in Gaul, Pompey, the conqueror of Palestine, had become the most powerful man in Rome. The Senators were on his side; preferring Pompey to Caesar, they elected Pompey as Consul.

In Gaul, Caesar was kept informed by his friends in Rome about what was going on, that more and more people took sides with Pompey, that soon Pompey would be so powerful that Caesar would have no chance against him. Yet, Caesar waited – he was not yet ready to start a war, a war in which Roman would fight Roman, a civil war. Even a man as ambitious as Caesar shrank from the thought of Romans fighting Romans.

The Senators and Pompey in Rome felt uneasy with Caesar in Gaul in command of a large army; all of these soldiers devoted to Caesar, all of them ready to fight for Caesar. Neither the Senators nor Pompey could feel entirely safe as long as Caesar had this army at his command. But Caesar was only a general, and a general is not a king, a general has to obey the government, and the Senators and Pompey as Consul *were* the government. So the Senators sent a message to Caesar, a message that was a command: "Disband your army, send your soldiers home, and return to Rome."

What should Caesar do? If he obeyed the Senators' command and came back to Rome alone, his life would be at the mercy of Pompey who might perhaps treat him generously, but never again would Caesar have a chance to gain power for himself. If Caesar disobeyed, he would be a rebel against his own government, and Roman soldiers led by Pompey would fight against him.

Caesar could not make up his mind what to do. He marched his army to a little river, called the Rubicon. This river was the borderline between Gaul and Italy. By this River Rubicon he had to make his decision. He could either order his troops to lay down their arms and return as private citizens to their homes in Italy. Or he could give them the order to march, fully armed, under his command across the bridge and that would mean rebellion and civil war.

Looking down upon the stream he stood for a long time, deep in thought, while the soldiers stood at a distance waiting for his command.

Now while Caesar and his army were on one side of that River Rubicon, there was, on the other side, a shepherd who began to play a tune on his flute. Some of Caesar's soldiers liked the shepherd's playing, and one of them said: "Let's run across the bridge to the other side, we can hear him better from nearby." And so a number of the soldiers ran over the bridge to the other side. And when Caesar saw some of his men cross the bridge, it seemed to him that this was a sign sent by the gods; he turned round to the waiting army and shouted with a loud voice: "The gods have sent a sign, the die is cast. March on soldiers, and cross the Rubicon."

Ever since it has been a metaphor to say of someone who made a great and difficult decision: he has "crossed the Rubicon."

# 34. Greetings, O King

Caesar had marched his troops across the Rubicon and into Italy. Then city after city in northern Italy opened their gates to him, the inhabitants came out to greet him, cheer him and welcome him. It was as if they had all been waiting for him.

In Rome itself there was great confusion when the news came that Caesar had defied the command of the Senators. Pompey quickly tried to gather an army, but to his dismay he found his own soldiers deserting him and joining Caesar's advancing army. When Pompey saw that he could not rely on any Italian troops, he decided to raise an army in Greece, where he had many supporters and friends. And so Pompey fled to Greece.

Thus it came about that Julius Caesar could march right through Italy into Rome without finding any opposition – not a sword was raised against him. When his soldiers marched into Rome they marched singing and the people of Rome cheered them. The Senators trembled in fear of their lives, and they were willing to do anything Caesar asked. He was appointed Consul, Tribune, even Dictator – anything to please him. Perhaps they thought it did not matter, that sooner or later Pompey would return and deal with Caesar for them. But they were mistaken. It was Caesar who eventually sailed with his army to Greece. And Pompey the Great, who had never lost a battle, lost the battle of Pharsalus, where he was defeated by Caesar.

Pompey escaped and found a ship which took him to Egypt. But the King of Egypt had no wish to shelter a man who was an enemy of Caesar. The King wanted to show himself as a friend of Caesar, and he showed it in a gruesome way. When ten days later, Caesar arrived with a legion of his troops he was given a royal welcome. And when Caesar asked about Pompey, the King of Egypt gave an order and a servant brought in Pompey's head. He had been killed. When Caesar looked at the head of the man who had once been his friend, who had been one of Rome's greatest generals, he broke down and wept.

But now that Pompey was dead Caesar had no longer any rival who could oppose him. He was the most powerful man in the whole Roman Empire.

He was by then 52 years old. When he returned to Rome, people remembered Sulla and they feared Caesar would revenge himself on the Senators, on Pompey's friends and on anyone who had opposed Caesar. But he surprised everybody, his friends and his enemies alike, by his leniency. He not only forgave Pompey's friends, but gave them high positions. He looked after the soldiers who had loyally stood by him and fought for him: each one received generous gifts of money as well as a plot of land in Italy. But he also looked after the poor of Rome, it was by Caesar's command that Carthage was rebuilt so that poor people from Rome and other cities of the Empire could make a new state with houses and gardens of their own in North Africa.

Strangely Caesar, besides being Consul, Tribune and Dictator, had been given another great honour – he was appointed *Pontifex Maximus,* the highest priest, the priest above all other priests. *(Pontifex* means bridge-builder, a priest is a man who builds a bridge between humans and the gods; the Latin name for the Pope is still *Pontifex).*

As the highest priest in the whole Roman Empire, Caesar had to deal with the calendar, to fix the dates of the Roman festivals. The Roman calendar up to the time of Caesar was not like ours. They went by the moon. It is about $29\frac{1}{2}$ days from one full moon to the next, and a month (the word comes from "moon") was only 29 or 30 days; Twelve months give 354 days $(29\frac{1}{2} \times 12)$ which is 11 days short of the real year. This meant that every new year started 11 days earlier than the year before – it was a great mess.

Caesar changed all that. He called some famous astronomers from Egypt, and with their advice the calendar was changed as it is now (except for a minor change in leap years which came later). The months were made longer – 30 or 31 days except February which kept its 28 days or 29 days every four years (a leap year). This gave a year of 365¹/₄ days. And in honour and memory of Caesar's new calendar, one bright and sunny month, was called July – the month of Julius (Caesar). The number of days in every month goes back to Julius Caesar, and when we speak of "July" we are still honouring the name of Julius Caesar.

Another honour given to Caesar was the title: Imperator. This meant he was supreme commander of all Roman soldiers anywhere. We still use the word "empire," which comes from *imperator*. So Caesar had reached a height of power such as no man had held before him: Dictator, Consul, Imperator, highest priest. Although he was ambitious and enjoyed being the most powerful man in Europe, he used his great powers wisely.

But there was one title Caesar did not have – that was the title King. He had more power than any king, but he could not call himself king. Even the Roman citizens who loved him would have turned against him if he had, because all the other powers and titles Caesar had would die with him – he could not pass them on to a son or to a relative. (He had no son, his near-est relative was a nephew, Octavius). But kingship goes by inheritance. And the Romans did not want any more kings; while they adored Caesar, when he died, Rome would be a republic again and not at the mercy of one man.

That was why the Romans would have turned against Caesar if he had assumed the title King. Caesar knew this, and he was very careful to avoid any suspicion that he also wanted to be king. But his own friends were not so careful, some of them thought he should be king. There was one young man, an officer who had fought for Caesar against Pompey, who admired Caesar very much. One day when Caesar came to the Forum, this young officer, Mark Antony, greeted him with the words: "*Ave, Rex*. Greetings, O King."

Caesar frowned and said: "Mark Antony, don't you know my name is Caesar, not King."

But from that day onwards there were rumours in Rome that Caesar wanted to be king. One day during the great festi-val, Lupercalia, Caesar watched the singing and celebrating people in the streets from a balcony, and the people saw him and cheered him. Then Mark Antony appeared on the balcony with a golden crown in his hand and he offered the golden crown to Caesar. When he did this the crowds fell silent, but Caesar smiled, shook his head and pushed the crown away. And when they saw this the crowds cheered wildly. Once again Mark Antony held out the crown and Caesar refused it, and a third time, and Caesar pushed it away, and the crowds cheered him.

But Caesar's enemies spread rumours that Mark Antony had only offered the crown to Caesar because Caesar himself had told him to, he wanted to find out how the Romans felt about him becoming a king. And a good many people in Rome began to believe in these whispers and rumours.

# 35. The Ides of March

At that time Rome was full of rumours: "Caesar is going to be proclaimed king." "No," said others, "the people will never stand for it." "Oh, his soldiers will stand by him, they will force us to accept him as king." People whispered and talked.

And even the people who loved Caesar began to believe that he was going to call himself king and would pass his power to his young nephew, Octavius. After all, why did Caesar take young Octavius with him wherever he went? Why did he treat Octavius like a crown prince?

And there were still people in Rome who, although they liked Caesar, did not want Rome to be forever under one man's rule. They hoped that when Caesar died Rome would be free to choose a leader. One of these people was a man called Brutus. He was a descendant of the Brutus who once drove out the last king, Tarquin, the Etruscan. Brutus had every reason to like Caesar, for Caesar was fond of him and had never refused Brutus any favour.

Brutus liked Caesar, but he believed with all his heart that Rome should become a republic again. He feared that Caesar would not rest until he was king and that would be the end of all hopes that the Romans would ever again be able to choose their leaders. Brutus became more and more convinced that there was only one way to stop Caesar – that was to kill him.

Although Brutus was a friend of Caesar, he felt it was his duty to Rome to kill Caesar before he proclaimed himself king. Now Brutus had a friend, Cassius who, unlike Brutus, hated Caesar. Cassius had been a friend of Pompey and he could not forget how miserably poor Pompey had died because of Caesar. It was true that Caesar had been kind to Cassius, and had even given him a high position, but in his heart Cassius had not for-given Caesar. He wanted to revenge Pompey.

And these two men, Brutus and Cassius found a number of other Romans who hated Caesar for all kinds of reasons – envy, ambition, revenge – and these conspirators came together secretly to plan and plot the murder of Caesar. But the more people who joined the conspiracy the greater was the danger that one of them would betray the others to Caesar. Brutus and Cassius decided they could not wait any longer: the time to strike had come.

On March 15 (the Romans called the middle a month the "Ides") there was to be an important meeting in the Senate in the Forum. Naturally Caesar would be there – and that would be the time and the place to kill him.

Now a soothsayer, a man who claimed that he could foresee the future, had warned Caesar that the Ides of March, March 15, would bring great danger, and he should be on his guard. But Caesar only laughed at this warning.

On the evening of March 14, there was a banquet in Caesar's house and during the conversation his guests began to talk about death. One of them asked Caesar what kind of death he would wish for himself. "A sudden death," answered Caesar. During the night Caesar's wife, Calpurnia, had a nightmare in which she saw Caesar's blood-stained body brought into the house. When she woke up next morning, she begged Caesar with tears not to go to the Senate on that day. And Caesar, to do her a favour, agreed to stay at home.

When Caesar did not arrive at the Senate, there was great consternation among the Senators. What should they do? Why had he not come? But more upset than the Senators were Brutus and Cassius and the other conspirators who had come with daggers hidden in their togas. And Brutus went to Caesar's house to find out what was keeping him. When Caesar told him of his wife's dream, Brutus said: "Shall I tell Rome that Caesar stays at home because of his wife's dreams?"

Of course this hurt Caesar's pride; he did not want the Romans to laugh at him, and in spite of his wife's desperate pleas he went away with Brutus.

As they walked through the streets Caesar saw the soothsayer who had prophesied evil would befall him on the Ides of March. Caesar called out "The Ides of March have come my friend."

"Yes" answered the soothsayer, "but they have not yet passed."

Among the people in the street there was a man who seemed eager to hand Caesar a piece of paper. "Read it, Caesar," he said, "it concerns your safety!" The paper contained the names of the men who had planned to kill Caesar. But Caesar was by now in a hurry to get to the Senate, so he did not look at the paper and gave it to somebody to hold it for him.

As soon as Caesar entered the Senate, Brutus, Cassius and the other conspirators closed around him so that the Senators and other people could not see what was going on. Then one of them handed Caesar a letter with a request which Caesar had once before refused. Caesar looked at the letter, was annoyed and spoke sharply to the man, then he turned away. At this moment the man took Caesar's toga at the back of his neck and pulled it down. This was the sign for the conspirators, they all drew their daggers and stabbed at Caesar.

With blood pouring from his wounds, Caesar struck with his bare hands at his assailants. But then he saw Brutus – the man whom he had liked and trusted, lift his dagger and strike at him. Caesar cried out, *"Et tu Brutus?* You too, Brutus?" Then he covered his face with his toga, fell to the floor and died.

That was the end of Caesar, the man who had gained more power than any Roman before him. When the Senators saw what had happened in the Senate, in the place of law and justice, they were horrified and fled. They did not want to have anything to do with it. As they ran from the Senate they met Mark Antony, the young officer who so greatly admired Caesar. When Mark Antony heard the horrible news he feared he too was to be murdered as a friend of Caesar and he also fled, but not for long.

In the meantime the conspirators, Brutus, Cassius and the others, held speeches in the Forum, telling the Romans they had killed the tyrant Caesar and brought freedom to Rome, but most people were as horrified as the Senators and hurried away.

Now the conspirators began to worry that the people of Rome might turn against them. They were still discussing what they should do, when Mark Antony came forward and demanded that Caesar should be given a public funeral. Brutus and Cassius agreed. At a public funeral it was the custom to make speeches, so this was an opportunity for them to speak to the people of Rome and to explain that they were not common murderers but had killed Caesar for the sake of Roman freedom. And they agreed that Mark Antony should also be allowed to speak.

On the next day Caesar's body was placed on a bier at the Forum. First Brutus spoke, and he spoke with such sincerity explaining why he, a friend of Caesar, had decided that Caesar had to die before he made himself king – he spoke so well that the people of Rome cheered him, and agreed that what Brutus had done was right. But then it was Mark Antony's turn. And his speech is immortalised in the words of the greatest English playwright, in the words of Shakespeare (*Julius Caesar* III,ii):

> Friends, Romans, countrymen, lend me your ears;
> I come to bury Caesar, not to praise him.
> The evil that men do lives after them,
> The good is oft interred with their bones;
> So let it be with Caesar. The noble Brutus
> Hath told you that Caesar was ambitious;
> If it were so, it was a grievous fault,
> And grievously hath Caesar answer'd it.
> Here, under leave of Brutus and the rest,
> For Brutus is an honourable man;
> So are they all, all honourable men;
> Come I to speak in Caesar's funeral.
> He was my friend, faithful and just to me:
> But Brutus says he was ambitious;
> And Brutus is an honourable man.
> He hath brought many captives home to Rome,
> Whose ransoms did the general coffers fill:
> Did this in Caesar seem ambitious?
> When that the poor have cried, Caesar hath wept;
> Ambition should be made of sterner stuff:

Yet Brutus says he was ambitious;
And Brutus is an honourable man.
You all did see that on the Lupercal
I thrice presented him a kingly crown,
Which he did thrice refuse: was this ambition?
Yet Brutus says he was ambitious;
And, sure, he is an honourable man.
I speak not to disprove what Brutus spoke,
But here I am to speak what I do know.
You all did love him once, not without cause:
What cause withholds you then to mourn for him?
O judgment! thou art fled to brutish beasts,
And men have lost their reason. Bear with me;
My heart is in the coffin there with Caesar,
And I must pause till it come back to me.

... [*the citizens come round to Antony's view*]

But yesterday the word of Caesar might
Have stood against the world; now lies he there,
And none so poor to do him reverence.
O masters! if I were disposed to stir
Your hearts and minds to mutiny and rage,
I should do Brutus wrong, and Cassius wrong,
Who, you all know, are honourable men.
I will not do them wrong; I rather choose
To wrong the dead, to wrong myself, and you,
Than I will wrong such honourable men.
But here's a parchment with the seal of Caesar;
I found it in his closet, 'tis his will.
Let but the commons hear this testament,
Which, pardon me, I do not mean to read,
And they would go and kiss dead Caesar's wounds,
And dip their napkins in his sacred blood,
Yea, beg a hair of him for memory,
And, dying, mention it within their wills,
Bequeathing it as a rich legacy
Unto their issue. ...

[*Calls to read the will*]

Have patience, gentle friends; I must not read it:
It is not meet you know how Caesar loved you.
You are not wood, you are not stones, but men;
And, being men, hearing the will of Caesar,
It will inflame you, it will make you mad.
'Tis good you know not that you are his heirs;
For if you should, O! what would come of it.

... [*More calls to read the will*]

Will you be patient? Will you stay awhile?
I have o'ershot myself to tell you of it.
I fear I wrong the honourable men,
Whose daggers have stabb'd Caesar; I do fear it.

... [*Brutus & Cassius are seen as traitors*]

You will compel me then to read the will!
Then make a ring about the corpse of Caesar,
And let me show you him that made the will.
Shall I descend? and will you give me leave?

... [*Room is made for him*]

If you have tears, prepare to shed the now.
You all do know this mantle: I remember
The first time ever Caesar put it on;
'Twas on a summer's evening, in his tent,
That day he overcame the Nervii.
Look! in this place ran Cassius' dagger through;
See what a rent the envious Casca made:
Through this the well-beloved Brutus stabb'd;
And as he pluck'd his cursed steel away,
Mark how the blood of Caesar follow'd it.
As rushing out of doors, to be resolved
If Brutus so unkindly knock'd or no;

For Brutus, as you know, was Caesar's angel:
Judge, O ye gods! how dearly Caesar loved him.
This was the most unkindest cut of all;
For when the noble Caesar saw him stab,
Ingratitude, more strong than traitor's arms,
Quite vanquished him; then burst his mighty heart;
And, in his mantle muffling up his face,
Even at the base of Pompey's statua,
Which all the while ran blood, great Caesar fell.
O! what a fall was there, my countrymen;
Then I, and you, and all of us fell down,
Whilst bloody treason flourish'd over us.
O! now you weep, and I perceive you feel
The dint of pity; these are gracious drops.
Kind souls, what! weep you when you but behold
Our Caesar's venture wounded? Look you here,
Here is himself, marr'd, as you see, with traitors.

... [*Citizens call for revenge*]

Good friends, sweet friends, let me not stir you up
To such a sudden flood of mutiny.
They that have done this deed are honourable:
What private griefs they have, alas! I know not,
That made them do it; they are wise and honourable,
And will no doubt, with reason answer you.
I come not, friends, to steal away your hearts:
I am no orator, as Brutus is;
But, as you know me all, a plain blunt man,
That love my friend; and that they know full well
That gave me public leave to speak of him.
For I have neither wit, nor words, nor worth,
Action, nor utterance, nor the power of speech,
To stir men's blood: I only speak right on;
I tell you that which you yourselves do know,
Show you sweet Caesar's wounds, poor poor dumb mouths,
And bid them speak for me: but were I Brutus,
And Brutus Antony, there were an Antony

Would ruffle up your spirits, and put a tongue
In every wound of Caesar, that should move
The stones of Rome to rise in mutiny.

... [*Citizens call for mutiny*]

Why, friends, you go to do you know not what.
Wherein hath Caesar thus deserved your loves?
Alas! you know not: I must tell you then.
You forgot the will I told you of.

... [*Call for will to be read*]

Here is the will, and under Caesar'seal.
To every Roman citizen he gives,
To every several man, seventy-five drachmas.
...
Moreover, he hath left you all his walks,
His private arbours, and new-planted orchards,
On this side Tiber; he hath left them you,
And to your heirs for ever; common pleasures,
To walk abroad, and recreate yourselves.
Here was a Caesar! when comes such another?

# 36. At Philippi

People who have been in danger of sudden death, for instance a mountaineer falling down a cliff, or a swimmer who was nearly drowned, but who have been saved at the last moment, have in many cases had a strange experience. They tell that they saw their whole life – all the events of their life from childhood onwards up to that moment – flash before them in a second. If this happens to people who have nearly died, it may well happen to everyone when they really die that they have a picture of their whole life when it comes to an end.

Just think of the moment when Caesar cried out, "You too Brutus!" and covered his face with his toga, and sank to the floor of the Senate. In that moment he perhaps saw his whole life – all the little and the great events of his life. What would he have seen?

He saw again the day when he stood before Sulla and was threatened with death if he did not divorce his plebeian wife, the day he recited poems to the pirates and they laughed at him, the day he made a pact with Crassus and Pompey, the dark forests of Gaul, the men of the Tenth Legion who adored him, the Rubicon where he had pondered what to do, his own triumph and the Senators giving him all the titles and honours they could, the battle against Pompey, that horrible day in Egypt when Pompey's head was shown to him, Mark Antony who loved him but had also – unwillingly – helped rumours against Caesar, his nephew Octavius, Brutus whom he had trusted and who was one of his murderers. It was a great, adventurous life that ended on March 15, 44 BC. It was a life that had led him to power – great power, and he had paid the price for it, in having enemies, in being hated.

With Caesar's death a new struggle for power began. Mark Antony had with his great speech, swayed the hearts of the

Romans so that they turned against the conspirators, Brutus and Cassius. Caesar's murderers had to flee from Rome, and they sailed to Greece. Brutus, despite having murdered Caesar who trusted him, did not want power for himself. He truly and sincerely wanted to bring back the Roman Republic. But Mark Antony, who had roused the Romans against Brutus, saw himself as Caesar's successor. Mark Antony wanted power.

But there was someone else who considered himself the rightful successor to Caesar. It was Octavius, Caesar's nearest male relative, his nephew. For a time it looked as if Mark Antony and Octavius were going to start a civil war. But when they heard that Brutus and Cassius had raised an army in Greece (there were always men in Greece ready to rebel against the Romans), they realised it would be madness if they fought a war against each other. They made a pact to join forces. The agreement was that they should first defeat Brutus and Cassius, and when that was done, they would share the Roman Empire between them as equal partners. Then their armies sailed across to Greece and marched through that land until they came in sight of the troops gathered by Brutus and Cassius. The place where the two armies came face to face was near a town called Philippi.

The night before the battle a strange thing happened to Brutus. He was alone in his tent, his soldiers were asleep except for the men who stood silently on guard through the night. It was very quiet, but Brutus could not sleep. It was not the battle next day which worried him, he was a Roman and battles were a part of life for a Roman. But since Caesar's death he found it difficult to sleep. And as he sat in his tent by the light of a little oil-lamp, he suddenly felt he was not alone, he looked up and there stood before him a strange, gaunt figure. "Who are you?" cried Brutus.

"I am your evil genius," spoke the apparition, and then Brutus recognised the ghost of Caesar.

He shouted, "What do you want of me?"

And the ghost answered with a hollow voice: "Tomorrow I will see you at Philippi."

But now Brutus pulled himself together and replied: "Well then, we shall meet at Philippi." And the ghost disappeared.

Brutus was no coward. Ghost or no ghost, he led his men so well and fought so courageously that Octavius' troops gave way and turned to flee. But Mark Antony, who had battled and won against Brutus' friend, Cassius, could now come to Octavius' rescue. That was the end of the battle, with Brutus' soldiers fleeing, and Brutus fleeing with them. Cassius had killed himself rather than surrender.

During the night Brutus realised that he could not escape – that Mark Antony and Octavius would not rest until they captured him and killed him for the murder of Caesar. But Brutus would not allow himself to be led in chains through Rome, a Roman was too proud for such an end. And so in that night after the battle of Philippi, Brutus killed himself by his own sword.

When Antony's soldiers found the body of Brutus, Mark Antony himself came, and looked in silence upon his dead enemy. Then he said, "Here lies a noble Roman," and put his own purple cloak over Brutus, as a sign of respect for a noble enemy.

Now Octavius and Antony kept their agreement, their pact. In the city of Rome and in Italy, they ruled together as equal partners. Outside Italy, Octavius was to rule Gaul and Spain in the West, Antony was to rule the East, Greece, Syria, Palestine. To seal the agreement and to strengthen their friendship, Mark Antony married Octavius' sister, Octavia.

However, the people of Rome, the Senators, no longer had any say. Antony and Octavius simply divided the power between themselves as they pleased. The Senators were just told, and had to agree. Brutus had killed Caesar in vain; he had lost his own life in vain. There was never again a Roman Republic.

# 37. Antony and Cleopatra

For a time Mark Antony stayed in Rome with his young wife, Octavia, and shared the task of ruling the great Roman Empire with Octavius. But Antony was eager to go to the lands in the East where he did not have to share power with Octavius. So he left his wife in Rome and went first to Greece. Many Greeks had been ready to fight for the luckless Brutus, and Antony made it his first task to punish the men who had helped Brutus. Many a Greek lost his life or languished in prison for having been on the losing side in the battle of Philippi.

But Antony found that not only Greeks had helped Brutus, soldiers had also been sent from Egypt to fight for Brutus. This was a serious matter. How could Egypt dare interfere in a quarrel between Romans? Who had sent Egyptian soldiers to support Brutus? Antony discovered that it was a woman, the Queen of Egypt (at that time there was no king in Egypt).

Antony did not bother to sail with an army from Greece across to Egypt, it would not need an army to teach this woman a lesson, Antony sent a messenger to the Queen of Egypt with a command: "Come to Tarsus in Syria, and explain why you have helped the murderers of Caesar."

The Queen of Egypt came. Only a few weeks after the command had been sent, Antony was informed that a ship was approaching – a ship, so his servants told him excitedly, such as no one had seen before. Driven by curiosity, Antony hastened to the harbour and saw an amazing sight. The royal Egyptian ship was covered with gold leaf so that it looked as if it were made of gold. The ship carried a sail of purple★ and the oars were studded with silver nails, they looked as if they were made of pure silver.

★ Purple dye was the rarest and most valuable colour made from a mollusc (the murex) found on the shores around Tyre and Sidon.

When this glittering vessel reached the pier, a gangway was laid down and a black slave invited Antony to come on board. Even in Rome Antony had never seen such splendour. He stepped onto the deck. There, reclining on a couch was the most beautiful woman he had ever seen: dark-haired, with large black eyes, her beautiful figure dressed in robes of finest silk; a servant fanned her with peacock feathers; around her musicians played softly on harps.

With a voice that sounded like music, the Queen invited him to sit down beside her. And this woman's beauty, charm and cleverness, worked like a magic spell on Antony. Within a few moments he forgot that he had summoned her to punish her, he forgot the young wife he had left in Rome, he forgot Rome and his duties and his pact with Octavius. Only one thing mattered to him: this beautiful woman, the Queen of Egypt, Cleopatra.

The next day the ship sailed back to Egypt, and with it went Antony. He went with Cleopatra to Alexandria, and there he stayed. The great Mark Antony who had defeated Brutus and Cassius, whose speech had swayed the Romans, the friend of Julius Caesar, became as soft wax in the hands of Cleopatra.

He lived in fantastic luxury and splendour in Cleopatra's palace as if he were her husband, and he gave no thought to his wife in Rome and how she suffered when she heard the news. His life was so filled with feasts, pleasures, amusements; he was so under the spell of Cleopatra that he cared not at all what happened in Rome.

But Octavius, Antony's partner, had in the meantime shown the Romans that he was a worthy successor to Caesar. The Roman legions were well trained and well paid, Roman law and Roman justice kept order and peace in the land. In the beginning the Romans had liked Antony better, for he was a handsome, dashing young officer, and could make rousing speeches. But in time they saw that Octavius, this rather earnest man who worked hard and took his task of governing Rome very seriously, was really, a better man and a better ruler than Antony.

In the end Octavius decided – and the citizens of Rome agreed – that he would no longer tolerate a partner who had deserted his wife, who did no work at all and spent his time

living in lazy luxury under the spell of a foreign queen. So
Octavius set out with a fleet to fight Antony and to end the
partnership. Antony was not worried – he had his own fleet,
and Cleopatra had a fleet of ships too, and insisted on com-
manding her fleet in battle.

So the joint fleets of Antony and Cleopatra clashed with the
ships of Octavius in the Mediterranean Sea, near the Greek
town of Actium. But in the midst of this sea-battle Cleopatra
quite suddenly ordered all her ships to turn back to Alexandria.
When Antony saw Cleopatra's ships sail away, he lost all interest
in the sea-battle, and sailed quickly after her, leaving the other
ships of his fleet to their fate: they were destroyed by Octavius.

Antony arrived in Alexandria, and was told by weeping servants that Cleopatra had killed herself. When he heard this he
was in such despair that, like Brutus, he killed himself by his
own sword. However, Cleopatra had deceived him, she was still
alive and hoped that now she would be able to cast her spell over
Octavius. But she was mistaken. When Octavius arrived in
Alexandria with his victorious fleet he put Cleopatra under a
guard of Roman soldiers. And Cleopatra soon found out from
the officer of the guard what was in store for her: to be led in
chains through the streets of Rome in Octavius' triumph. When
she heard that, Cleopatra knew that she had no hope of catching
Octavius in her net. At her request, the Roman guards gave permission for one of her servants to bring her a basket of figs.
Hidden under the figs were poisonous snakes. Cleopatra took a
snake and let it bite her.

Thus the most beautiful woman of her time died. When
Octavius heard of her death he only regretted that she would
not be in his triumph in Rome.

# 38. God on Earth

How different the two men were who had wanted to take the place of Julius Caesar, Antony and Octavius. Antony was a dashing officer, strong, handsome, who could talk eloquently; he was a man whom everybody liked at first sight. But his pleasant exterior was only exterior, for inside he was weak and soft, pursuing pleasure and luxury while duty, hard work and responsibility were of little concern to him. If you had met Antony you might have liked him, but you could never respect him.

Octavius was the opposite, despising luxury. Even when he reached the highest office in Rome, his meals were those of a simple Italian peasant: plain bread, cheese, olives, very little meat, a little wine. He could have worn the finest clothes money could buy, but he chose a tunic and a toga hand-woven by his wife, Livinia, on her own loom. She, too, could have had the luxury of a queen, but she preferred to live like a simple Roman housewife. If you had met Octavius, you would not have taken a liking to him immediately, he would have seemed too serious, too earnest, a man of few words; he was not an amusing companion like Antony. You might have found him a cold person, not as lively as Antony, but in time you would have found that this quiet man had enormous inner strength and iron determination. You may not have liked him, but you had to respect him.

It was therefore no accident or luck that in the end it was Octavius who took Caesar's place. Antony was bound to have lost, destroyed by his own weakness. It was certainly a good thing for Rome that Octavius came to power, for he did not misuse his power for an easy life of luxury. He took his duties as ruler of a great empire very seriously and worked harder and longer hours than many a rich man in Rome. He proved himself a wise ruler, and for the first time in many years Rome was free of civil war, there was peace in the land, and trade and business prospered. It was also the time when great poets flourished, like Virgil, a great writer at the time of Octavius. The Romans themselves called this time the Golden Age of Rome.

Octavius did not want the title Dictator, and he knew that the Romans did not like the title King, and so he thought of a new title for the rulers of Rome, the name of his uncle: Caesar. From then onwards, the title of a Roman ruler was Caesar.

But the Romans were so happy to have a wise, just ruler, that the Senators honoured him by giving him a new name: instead of Octavius he was called Augustus, he became Caesar Augustus. Now this name Augustus was a very special name because it was a word that had up to that time only been used for gods. Augustus means "he who brings good fortune," and the Romans used to speak of their god Jupiter as Jupiter Augustus, Jupiter who brings good fortune.

But now this word Augustus that had only been used for gods – for only a god could send good fortune – was used for a man. By giving him the name Augustus the Romans were saying: we think of you as a godlike being.

Romans had the feeling that the more power you have, the more you are like the gods. And Octavius, or Caesar Augustus as he was now called, was certainly the most powerful man in the world. No wonder that they thought of him as a godlike being. In his honour the month after July, the next sunny month, was called August. Roman history can still be seen in our calendar.

Now Caesar Augustus had a great knowledge of things that had happened in times long past. He knew, for instance, that in ancient Egypt, the god Osiris had ruled as king, as Pharaoh. It would be good for the Romans – he thought – if they, like the ancient Egyptians, looked up to their rulers as gods.

Caesar Augustus saw nothing wrong in letting himself be called a god. Soon temples were built in which stood the statue of Caesar Augustus, and the Romans came quite happily and made sacrifices before these statues and worshipped them. From that time on it became a custom, and the Caesars who came after him were also worshipped as gods. Caesar Augustus was the first who made the Romans worship him as a god.

Yet at the time when this man – Octavius, the nephew of Julius Caesar – set himself up as a god, in far away Palestine something tremendous happened: God became man in Jesus Christ. The Jesus child was born at the time of Caesar Augustus.

The Christ-child was born in a stable; Mary and Joseph could not find room in any inn: the true divine child was born in a small village, in Bethlehem, in poverty, in a land crushed and conquered by the Romans.

At that time, when God became truly man in Jesus Christ, in Rome a man, Caesar Augustus, set himself up as a god. In Rome people worshipped a man as a god; in faraway Palestine God became man and only a few people, a few poor shepherds and the wise men, came to worship the little child.

In one other place were there people who knew that something tremendous had happened in a far away land. In Britain, especially in Ireland, there were still Druids who said: something has happened – the holy wisdom that was in the sunlight has come to earth.

But Rome knew only power, and worshipped the most powerful man, Caesar Augustus, as a god.

# 39. In Palestine and in Rome

Often, though not always, children have a likeness to their fathers or their mothers. If you see the parent and the child together you will notice that there is a certain likeness. And it is not only a likeness in looks, sometimes a talent for art, for drawing, for music, or for numbers, is in one of the parents and also in the child. This is also a likeness, something the child has inherited from father or mother.

We all have our own fathers and mothers, but there is also our great Father in heaven, God, and all human beings are His children. But God is a spirit, he is not a being of flesh and blood like our parents. Yet, we can also show a likeness to our heavenly Father. It is not in our looks, we cannot look like Him – He is spirit; we cannot show it by our cleverness, for no human being can have a wisdom that is like God's. The Romans felt power makes you akin to God, but no human being has the power to create a world as God has. Neither by our little human wisdom nor by our little power (we can destroy life, but cannot make life), can we show that we have a likeness to God, that we are all God's children.

But God is really love, pure love, and the more we show love, kindness and friendship to all human beings, to all that lives and is, the more we show our likeness to the heavenly Father. We show our likeness to God, that we are truly children of the Father in Heaven, by every deed of love and kindness.

At the time of the Romans, the souls and minds of people on earth had become so dark, that all they knew of God was His power – they thought power made you godlike. And if this had continued mankind would have become worse and worse; cruelty, bloodshed, murder would have become more and more common if they helped you to have power. Think of the gladiator games, where men were made to kill each other, for the amusement of the spectators. Just think of the slaves who could be killed by their master, for he had the right to do so. All these evil and horrible things would have gone on, and they would even have become worse, if nothing new had happened to help humankind.

But something did happen. Humankind was saved from becoming ever more cruel and mad for power. Far away from the splendour and glitter of Rome, in the small, despised province of Palestine, Jesus was born. This child grew up in humble surroundings, his father Joseph was a poor carpenter in the town of Nazareth, and for thirty years Jesus lived quietly with his family among his people, the Jews. But at the age of thirty a great change came in his life.

At that time there was a wise man, a prophet, whose name was John. And John prophesied that a man of God would come and turn the minds of people on earth from their evil ways to the true light of God. He would be the Saviour. And all people who believed that God would send a saviour came to this prophet, John, and he baptised them in water of the holy River Jordan that flows through Palestine.

At the age of thirty Jesus came to John at the River Jordan to be baptised. At the moment when John baptised Jesus, the greatest event in the whole history of mankind happened. For at that moment the spirit of God that is pure love became one with Jesus. And Jesus became the Saviour, the Anointed One, which in Greek is *Christos.* Jesus became Christ, the Saviour.

From that moment when the spirit of God, that is love, became one with him, Christ preached to the people. He taught them that God is love. And once when He was asked: what is the most important rule for life? He answered: "Love each other human being on earth as if he were yourself, and love God more than anything else in the world."

But Jesus Christ not only preached love; the spirit of love was so strong and mighty in Him that it was like a force: when blind, lame and sick people were brought to Him and He touched them with His hands, the power of love that flowed through His hands healed them.

What was happening in Rome while these things happened in Palestine? In Rome, Caesar Augustus died after a long reign. As he had no son he was followed by his nephew, Tiberius, who became Caesar Tiberius. At first this new Caesar seemed a worthy successor of Augustus, he carried on the wise, just rule of Augustus. But after about seven years a terrible change came over Tiberius, it was as if a strange madness had taken hold of him. He began to imagine that he was surrounded by enemies who wanted to murder him. He kept a special bodyguard, soldiers who had only one duty: to protect him and to kill his enemies. He would not touch any food or drink unless a slave had first tasted it, in case it was poisoned. That the slave might die, did not matter to Caesar Tiberius.

But this was only the beginning of the madness. He began to imagine that his own relatives planned to murder him, and so his cousins, nephews, uncles were taken by the bodyguard and, without any trial, without a chance to protest their innocence, they were killed. The madness got worse. If the Romans praised a general for his victories, that general was executed at the order of Tiberius. If Senators or rich Romans became popular, they were killed at the order of Tiberius.

And the madness got worse, Caesar Tiberius began to hate the whole of mankind, he hated all human beings so much that he did not even want to see them. He left Rome, and had a great palace built for himself on the high cliffs of a little island, Capri, near Naples. There in that palace Tiberius lived with only his bodyguard and some old servants who had served him since his youth.★ No one else was allowed to approach the island of Capri on pain of death. A poor fisherman driven by a storm to the island was killed by the bodyguard who threw him down from a high cliff. Yet, during all that time Romans worshipped and offered sacrifices to the god Caesar Tiberius, for that had now become a law. They worshipped a madman, a figure of hate, a man who hated all mankind, while in Palestine Jesus spoke of God who is love, and preached the love of all humankind.

★ Selma Lagerlöf's story, "Faustina," from *The Emperor's Vision and other Christ Legends,* tells of the end of Tiberius' life.

In the end Tiberius became more suspicious than ever before, he would not even trust his bodyguard and had some of his soldiers executed. Then the other soldiers of the bodyguard decided they would not give Tiberius a chance to execute more of them. One morning a soldier went into the Emperor's bedroom and killed him by putting a pillow on his face and holding it down until he suffocated.

# 40. Caesars and Christians

When Pompey conquered Palestine, the Jews, the people of Palestine, did not become Romanised like, for instance, the Gauls: the Jews did not take on Roman customs, they refused to worship Roman gods, they refused later to worship the new gods Caesar Augustus and Caesar Tiberius. The Jews hated the Roman oppressors; they wished and hoped that a great leader, a great warrior, would rise among them to drive out the Romans.

When Jesus began His great work, people saw that He had powers such as no mortal man had ever possessed, that a touch of His hand would cure every illness and there were many Jews who thought that Jesus should lead them against the Romans, that he should use his powers to shatter the Roman legions. But the Spirit of God, the Spirit of Love had not come to earth for one nation, the Jews, but for all mankind so that human hearts should change, should no longer feel hatred and people should forgive their enemies.

Some Jews understood that new and wonderful force of love that came into the world through Jesus Christ and they followed Him as disciples, but most Jews hated the Romans so bitterly that they did not want to hear the message of Jesus. They did not want to forgive the Romans. And when they saw that Jesus was not going to lead them against the Romans, they turned against Jesus and hated Him too.

The greatest event in the history of the world had happened, the Spirit of God, the Spirit of Love had come, but human souls were in such darkness – hatred is really a darkness of the soul – that only a few people could at first recognise the wonderful thing that had come to Earth in Jesus. The others turned against Jesus; the Romans turned against Him for they feared He might lead a rebellion against them and the Jews turned against him because He would not lead them against the Romans. Only a few Jews and a few Romans could recognise the Spirit of God in Jesus.

But both the Jews and the Romans paid a heavy price for their blindness, for the darkness of hatred in their souls. The unhappy Jews paid their price thirty-seven years after that Good Friday when the crosses had been put up on the hill of Golgotha outside Jerusalem. Thirty-seven years later a leader came among the Jews who claimed that he was sent by God to drive out the Romans, and the Jews rose in rebellion against the Romans. But that man, Bar Kochba, had no powers and the Jewish rebellion came to a terrible end. The Jews fought with desperate courage, women, children, old men hurled themselves against the Roman legions, but all that desperate courage was of no avail against the might of Rome. A great number of Jews were killed in the fighting, the great Temple in Jerusalem where Jesus had preached went up in flames, only one foundation wall of it can still be seen today. And when the fighting was over, the Romans imposed a terrible punishment on the remaining Jews. The strongest men were taken away as slaves to Rome. Many others were driven out of Palestine: they were sent to Greece, Egypt, Spain, Italy, and so they lost their land, the Promised Land, to which Moses had brought their forefathers. What disaster the blind hatred of the Romans brought upon the unhappy Jews.

The Romans who believed in power, who would look upon their powerful Emperors, the Caesars, as gods, they paid their price in a different way, they were shown what kind of gods, what kind of divine beings, these Caesars were.

After Tiberius had been killed by his own bodyguard, he was succeeded by a nephew who had somehow been spared when Tiberius killed his relatives. The new Caesar was called Caligula, and Caligula was even more mad than Tiberius. He was not satisfied that Romans should worship his statue. Sometimes he dressed himself up as the god Jupiter, and the people of Rome had to worship him as Jupiter. At other times he dressed himself up as the goddess Venus, the goddess of beauty, and the Romans had to worship him as Venus.

One day Caligula decided that his favourite horse, a white stallion, would make an excellent Consul of Rome. And by that time the Senators, who had become so useless that they dare not refuse, appointed Caligula's horse as Consul of Rome. But by then Caligula's bodyguard thought such a mad man was not fit to rule, and they killed Caligula.

The next Caesar was a weak fool, Claudius, who could not rule at all and left all decisions and all government to his wife, Agrippina. Claudius and Agrippina had a son, and when he was seventeen years old, Agrippina thought she would have even more power if not her husband, but her son were Emperor. Suddenly her husband, Claudius, died – and there were whispers in Rome that his wife had poisoned him.

So Nero, the son of Claudius and Agrippina, became Caesar. He was the worst and most blood-thirsty monster in Roman history. He once said, "What a pity that all mankind has not just one head, then I could cut it off with one stroke."

One of his first deeds as Caesar was that he had his mother killed – he thought she was too tyrannical and the people of Rome had to celebrate a day of thanksgiving for this horrible deed.

Nero was not only a monster of cruelty, he was also exceedingly vain. He imagined that he had a beautiful voice and that he was a great singer. He would invite patricians and Senators to a banquet, then take a lyre and accompany himself singing to them. If any one of his audience did not applaud loudly enough or looked bored, Nero would have him arrested the next day and executed. The same happened to anybody who did not come when Nero invited him.

So Nero could always be sure to have a large audience and great applause. Sometimes he treated the people of Rome to his songs, they found it safer to clap loudly. At other times he would lay on hundreds of gladiators fighting each other in the circus for the amusement of the Romans. Sometimes hundreds of wild animals, lions, tigers, leopards were made to fight each other in the circus. They were kept hungry for days and then made even wilder with red-hot irons.

Yet, while all this cruel madness went on, something of much more importance happened in Rome. The apostles Peter and Paul had come to Rome and they found men and women who were eager to hear the message of Christ, the message that God is Love and that in loving each other we do the will of God.

So while most people in Rome enjoyed the cruelties of the shows provided by mad Nero, there were also good people who turned away from these horrors. Some who became Christian were slaves and some were rich and noble Romans. At first the other Romans took little notice of these Christians, but then something happened that changed all this. Nero wanted to be remembered as a great builder, and wanted to erect magnificent temples, palaces and great public baths with pools of hot and cold water. But at that time Rome was densely built up and there was little room for more building. The slums of Rome were ugly, dirty tenements where the poor people lived. If Nero could get rid of the slums there would be space for new, splendid buildings.

It was in July, the hottest, driest month in Rome. All rich people as well as Nero and his court had left Rome to stay in villas on the hills outside the city. And then, one night, several fires broke out at the same time in the slums of Rome. The wind spread the flames with terrible speed – ten out of fourteen districts of Rome were on fire. It is not known how many people lost their lives that night, certainly many thousands, and hundreds of thousands were made homeless. Nero could see Rome burning from his villa on the hills; he called his courtiers together, and while they watched the red sky and the sea of flames Nero played his lyre and sang a song comparing the burning of Rome with the burning of Troy.

However, during the following days the hundreds of thousands of homeless Romans began to wonder how the fire had started, and more and more of them cried out that Nero had sent men to set Rome ablaze. Nero was terrified that the Romans would turn against him – whom could he blame for the fire? Why not the Christians? They worshipped Jesus, a criminal who had died on the cross, they must themselves be criminals, wicked people. And so his men spread the rumour and soon the cry went through Rome: "the Christians have set fire to Rome, death to the Christians!"

Nero's soldiers marched through the streets and arrested hundreds of Christians. It was easy; they only had to ask: "Are you a Christian," and none of them, even though they knew what was in store for them, would deny their faith. They answered: "Yes, praise be to God, I am a Christian." They were brought to the great dungeons underneath the Circus Maximus, the great Circus of Rome. The persecution of the Christians had begun; the battle between the powers of evil – the Roman Caesars – and the God of Love had begun. And in this battle the God of Love fought with no other weapons but love and faith.

# 41. The Arena

Think back to ancient India where the five sons of Pandu who gave up their kingdom in search of the Kingdom of Heaven, were not afraid of leaving earth. They were looking forward to entering the world of the gods. The ancient Persians, who were much more at home on earth, still looked forward to the Kingdom of Light, the Kingdom of Ahura Mazda, when they died. But it was already different for Gilgamesh in ancient Babylon: after death there was only a dark, joyless life, and he feared death so much that he went in search of the plant of ever-lasting life. Later the Greeks felt that after death the soul is only a kind of shadow in the dark underworld. The world where human souls are after death had become dark, so dark that the soul of dead Achilles said to Odysseus: "Better a beggar on earth than a king in the dark underworld."

The coming of Christ was the most important, and greatest event in the whole history of humankind, not only for the people living on earth, but even for the souls of the dead. For when Jesus Christ's body was taken from the cross and laid in the tomb, the spirit of Christ, filled with God's power of love, appeared to the souls of the dead and brought light. The darkness was gone, and the Kingdom of Light, the Kingdom of Heaven opened for them again.

So for the early Christians – the Jews and the Romans who had taken the teaching of Christ into their hearts – a wonderful thing happened: through their faith in Christ they could feel that after death they would enter the Kingdom of Light and Love and Truth, the Kingdom of Heaven, and not a dark under-world. And as they knew this in their hearts, they had no fear of death at all.

As we heard, Nero blamed the burning of Rome on the Christians, and many hundreds of them were taken prisoner by his soldiers and thrown into the dungeons under the Circus Maximus in Rome. And then came the great day which Nero called "the day of revenge for the burning of Rome."

Already in the morning the great circus which could seat about 250,000 people began to fill. The Romans came, bringing with them food and drink to last them till nightfall. More and more people came; friends shouted greetings across the tiers; there was talking, shouting, laughter. But then came a hush. Nero and his court arrived and took their special seats. He looked fat, lazy and cruel, and the wreath on his head did not make him more handsome.

Now that Caesar Nero has arrived, the trumpets sounded, as a sign that the show could begin. And what a show! Driven with whips and lashes from their dungeons, the Christians were marched in procession round the circus. The crowds of specta-tors expected the Christians would either cry out for mercy – or show proud defiance. But instead, the Christians took no notice of the crowd. Steadily they made the round of the great circus and sang; they sang a psalm: The Lord is my Shepherd. And then they spoke a prayer, and the astonished Romans heard them say: "Our Father who art in heaven," and they heard them say: "Forgive us our tresppasses as we forgive our trespassers."

But now the Romans became impatient, and shouted: "Get on with the show!" The Christians were driven out again, for they were not to be killed together but in groups. When the arena was empty again there came a trumpet blast, and the real show began.

First a herd of big black bulls was driven into the arena, with Christian men and women tied to their horns. The bulls tried to get rid of the burdens on their heads, and they did in the end when there was no life left in the poor human bodies they had carried. The circus attendants drove the bulls away and cleared the arena. Another trumpet blast, Another group of Christians was driven into the Arena. They huddled together, praying. Another door opened and fierce lions, mad with hunger, came into the arena, and in a short time the arena was a shambles.

When darkness fell, the terrible performance came to an end. There was no street-lighting in Rome; if you were rich, a slave carried a burning torch for you, if you were poor you carried your own torch. But that night Rome had street-lighting, for all along the road Christians tied to crosses and covered with straw, were set alight and burning. But even as they died in flames, the Romans heard them pray as Jesus had prayed: "Father forgive them for they know not what they do."

But a strange thing happened: among the spectators who had come to these cruel shows, there were not just a few but many, many who thought: "The god whom these Christians worship has given them strength and courage beyond ordinary human powers – they went to their death without fear. We saw many of them die smiling as if a great joy was awaiting them. Surely their god must be the true god."

The Romans who thought thus searched for Christians who had escaped Nero's soldiers, and heard from them Christ's message of love, and became Christian themselves. So the Christians who had died in the Arena made more Christians and brought more Romans to the God of Love. The blood of the martyrs (as they were called) became the seed of the faith.

Just as Christ had risen from the dead, so the Christian faith rose from the dead martyrs and grew and spread, as the seed dies in the earth and a new ear of wheat, a new plant grows.

But now the Christians no longer met openly. Secretly they dug long, deep tunnels under the earth. These tunnels were called Catacombs; the entrances was cleverly hidden, and inside these tunnels or catacombs, the Christians buried their dead, and met and worshipped and held their divine services. These catacombs and the inscriptions made by the first Christians can still be seen today.

But Nero, the cruel monster, died as he deserved to die. In the end the legions in Gaul and Italy rose in rebellion against him. Nero fled from Rome, too cowardly to fight, and killed himself before his enemies could catch him.

The Caesars with all their might and riches destroyed themselves. But the Christian faith, without power or armies, without using swords even to defend itself, grew and spread and in the end triumphed over the Caesars.

# Early History of Britain and the Fall of the Roman Empire

# 42. The Stone Ages

The Roman times were about two thousand years ago. If you take about thirty years from parents to children, from one generation to the next, two thousand years are about seventy generations. But we want to go back much further – about ten thousand years – more than three hundred generations. When we go back as far as that, ten thousand years – or three hundred generations – we come to a time when our ancestors did not live in Britain: it was the time of Atlantis. And Britain was covered with ice, it was the ice age.

But it grew warmer and the ice began to melt. Seeds carried by the wind from warmer lands could germinate, and plants and trees began to grow. Slowly great forests grew and birds and animals came from warmer lands in the south.

These animals were still quite different from any you can see today: there were bison, stags much bigger than today's, enormous great bears, wild, shaggy horses, and a kind of elephant with long, shaggy fur, called a mammoth, even a kind of thick-furred tiger.

At that time, towards the end of the ice age, Britain was not yet quite cut off from the Continent by the Channel. It was still connected with the Continent, enabling these animals to come across, and in time also people to migrate.

These men and women were dressed in animal-skins held together by thongs, and they did not even build any kind of house, but sheltered in caves. But they had already mastered two great arts: they used fire for cooking, knowing how to ignite tinder (like dry moss) with sparks from flint-stones, and they knew how to make tools and weapons from flint-stones. But these first stone weapons and tools were still crude things; a sharp heavy stone tied to a stick was used as an axe. Flint was struck with another stone until there was a sharp-edge and a pointed splinter that could be used as a spear-head, an arrow-head, or as a knife.

This time is called the stone age, the age when people only had stone for tools and weapons. But with these crude weapons the stone age people hunted the great beasts, the bears, tigers, the mammoth, and hunted stags and buffalo.

These stone age hunters had a wonderful sense of beauty. With their sharp-edged stones they carved pictures of animals on bones, and, with red earth, they drew animal-pictures on the walls of their caves. In Britain we have no such paintings left, but in the South of France are the famous caves of Lascaux where the walls are covered with wonderful life-like paintings of bison and wild horses.

There is in fact not just one stone age, there are two: the first is called the old stone age, palaeolithic (from the Greek *palaeos,* old and *lithos,* stone), which we have just heard about, and then there is also a new stone age, neolithic.

After about two to three thousand years (we don't know exactly) a new people came to Britain, probably from Turkey or Persia. They brought with them new arts and skills. The new stone age, the neolothic, begins with these people. They had much greater skill in making their stone weapons and tools which were made smooth and sharp by grinding them with wet sand. They no longer lived in caves, but dug pits in the earth surrounded by an earth wall, with a roof of branches and twigs supported by a wooden pole.

Some of these neolithic people built wooden houses on branches or tree trunks driven into the bed of shallow lakes (many thousands of years later people did the same thing in Venice). These lake-dwellers also had dugouts, boats made of hollowed out tree-trunks. These neolithic people did not depend so much on hunting, but had tamed (or domesticated) animals. They had herds of cattle which they kept grazing near their dwellings, so they did not have to roam far and wide to hunt.

But the most important achievement of the new stone age people was that they planted seeds of wheat, barley and oats in fields near their dwellings, and harvested the grain when it was ripe. This was the beginning of agriculture, of farming. The new stone age is also the time of ancient Persia, when agriculture first started.

It was still primitive farming: the seeds were scattered on the ground and then sheep walked over them treading them into the earth. Threshing was done with sticks or by oxen walking over the ears of wheat. And then the grains were ground between two stones.

They no longer dressed in animal skins; in their fields they grew a plant called flax. The fibres of this plant were twisted into threads (we call it spinning) and the threads were woven on handlooms into a rough cloth, linen. The neolithic people wore linen clothes.

Another art of new stone age people was making pots, jars and jugs from wet clay and hardening them by fire. The old stone age people were still hunters, but the people of the new stone age were settled farmers who had new skills and arts.

# 43. The Bronze Age

A great change came in the neolithic, the new stone age, with the people who brought new arts and skills which had their origin in ancient Persia. Another change that came was the way people worked. During the palaeolithic, the old stone age, every man had to do every job for himself and his family: he skinned the animals and made these skins into the garments for himself and his family. But in the neolithic there were so many things to do – planting, ploughing and harvesting; building, making canoes and nets for fishing; looking after herds and milking cows; weaving, spinning and making pottery – so that one person, or even one family, could not do all of these jobs. So people divided the work between themselves: some would make stone tools and they became very skilled at it, some would tend the fields, others would hunt and fish, others again would build, or spin and weave. And the man who made stone tools would barter his spearheads and knives for the food brought by the hunter or produced by the farmer. This was the beginning of business. The "division of labour" was a great change, which we have to an even greater extent today. This division of labour began in the the neolithic which was also the time of ancient Persia. It is really the beginning of civilisation, for the division of labour leads to trade and business.

Wherever there was a community of neolithic people there was among them one group of men who were held in the greatest respect, who were regarded with great awe. These were the priests. They were very wise men, for they were doctors who knew herbs and ointments for every illness, they were the law-givers and settled any arguments between the people, and they knew how the sun and the moon and the stars change their places in the sky in the course of the year. All the sowing, planting and harvesting was done when the priests determined the right time of sun, moon and stars. Theirs was a kind of religion-science.

Under the guidance of these wise priests the people also made special tombs for their dead. Two or three stone-slabs were put upright, then a flat stone was put on top of them. The dead person was put inside and with him were put his possessions: weapons, ornaments, clay jars. Then the whole thing was covered with earth, forming a kind of earth-mound called tumulus. Many of these tumuli have been found in Britain and from the weapons and other things discovered inside much has been learnt about these people's way of life.

Under the guidance of these priests, even greater things were done. Not only were seeds sown in the fields in accordance with the position of sun, moon and stars, but all things in life were regulated by the priests in accordance with the sun and the moon. There was the right time to build a house, or the right time for a marriage feast. These people wanted the blessing of sun, moon and stars in all things they did, so it was very important to them to observe how sun, moon and stars changed their position in the sky in the course of the year.

To help the priests in observing these changes, the neolithic people built circles of stones. Standing in the middle of the circle at sunrise you could see how, from day to day, the place where the sun rose changed from one stone to another. And you could see the same changes for the moon and for certain groups of stars. The largest of these stone circles which we can still see in Britain was the stone circle of Stonehenge on Salisbury Plain in the South of England.

The people of the neolithic were no longer nomads and hunters (as the old stone age people had been), they had houses, fields and herds, and made clothes and pottery, and they looked up to sun, moon and stars to guide them in all they did on earth. The divine wisdom which guides the movements of the stars in heaven should also guide all they did on earth. And for this they built the great stone circles such as Stonehenge.

When Stonehenge was built, the climate and general conditions in Britain had changed very much. It had become much warmer, the great beasts like the mammoth, the bison, the giant bear, the giant elks, had all disappeared. Although there were still great forests with wolves, foxes and deer, there were already many larger and smaller human settlements all over Britain. And the sea-level had risen, cutting off Britain from the Continent.

But now a new people came across the Channel, the Celts. The Celts also came from the southeast – it is thought that they used to live around the Caspian Sea before they migrated northwards. Some of them settled in Central Europe, some in France but some went on and came to Britain about four thousand years ago. The time when the Celts came to Britain is also the time when Egyptian civilisation flourished, with its pyramids, hieroglyphics and mummies.

The Celtic people brought with them something quite new – their tools and weapons were not made of stone, but of bronze. The art of making bronze had been invented in Egypt. Egyptian priests had shown their people that if rocks which had veins of copper (that is, copper ore) were placed over a hot fire, the copper would melt and run down to the bottom of the fire. Then one could take the copper, heat it again and pour it into moulds to give it any shape: spear-heads, arrow-heads, swords, knives. But copper by itself is too soft for making sharp, useful tools and so a small amount of another metal, tin was added. And this stronger and harder mixture, or alloy, of copper and tin is called bronze.

This Egyptian invention had spread to other parts of the world, and the Celts had learned the art of extracting copper from ore, mixing it with tin and casting the bronze into moulds shaped like swords or spear-heads or ornaments. The Celts loved to decorate their weapons and specially their bronze shields; they made the most intricate spiral designs on shields and helmets and scabbards. With the coming of the Celts the stone age came to an end, and the bronze age began. As the Celts had much better bronze weapons than the neolithic people, the Celts became masters of Britain. But the holy places of the stone age people, the stone-circles where the movements of sun and moon and stars could be observed, remained holy places for the Celts. Now their priests, the druids, watched the course of the lights of heaven and guided the people in their life and work.

# 44. The Iron Age

Let us see how the civilisations of India, Persia and so on, go together with the "ages."

| | | |
|---|---|---|
| Ice age | Atlantis | Approx. 10,000 years ago |
| Palaeolithic | India | Approx. 8,000 years ago |
| Neolithic | Persia | Approx. 6,000 years ago |
| Bronze age | Egypt & Babylonia | Approx. 4,000 years ago |
| – | Greece and Rome | Approx. 2,000 years ago |

What is the "age" that corresponds to the times of ancient Greece and ancient Rome? The bronze age came to Britain with the first Celts, who had grey eyes and fair or brown hair, and who brought bronze tools and weapons to Britain. They were great artists and decorated their shields and swords with beautiful spiral ornaments. This bronze age lasted for about two thousand years: then, about five hundred years before the birth of Christ, new invaders came across the sea to Britain. These invaders were also Celts, but they had blue eyes and red hair. These new Celts, who came at the time when Greek and then Roman civilisation arose, had learned the use of a new metal, iron, for tools and weapons. The time of Greece and Rome, the time when the red-haired Celts came to Britain is the time when the iron age begins.

Using iron is quite different from the making of bronze weapons. The copper in bronze can easily be melted and cast in a mould. But it needed a much greater heat for iron to become red-hot and just soft enough to be hammered into shape, not poured into a mould like bronze.

In those ancient days when the iron age began, the smith, who forged red-hot iron and hammered it into shape on his anvil while fiery sparks flew around him, was regarded as a kind of magician who had command of strange powers. With the invention of iron tools and iron weapons humankind started on the long road which has led to railways, cars, planes, and also to guns and bombs. So perhaps the people who thought that the smith was a magician, had a feeling that with the use of iron a great power for good or for evil had been placed in human hands.

Iron tools and weapons were much harder than bronze. An iron sword was much sharper than a bronze sword, and lasted much longer. And so people soon gave up working in bronze and turned to iron. The beautiful bronze shields and weapons disappeared, and iron tools and weapons came which were not as beautiful as the bronze ones but much more practical. The iron age became less and less concerned with beauty, and as time went by more and more concerned only with practicality and usefulness.

Another great change came with the iron age. Until then people had bartered one thing for another, for instance exchanging cloth for clay-pots, or some grain for a knife. But in the iron age people began to use money, metal coins (not paper money there came again which came much later). At first they used little iron bars or bronze bars, but later they found round coins more practical, and gold, silver and bronze coins were used for buying and selling. The iron age is also the age of money.

It was the Celts who first used bronze and then iron in Britain. The Celts were a fiercely independent, proud and war-like people. Like the Greeks they were never united in one nation, and one tribe was forever fighting another.

Each tribe would build a fort with ditches and ramparts on top of a hill where they could see approaching enemies from afar, and where it was difficult for enemies to attack. You can still see remains of such a Celtic hill-forts from the iron age.

It was these endless quarrels between the Celtic tribes which helped the Romans conquer Britain when they came. When in 54 BC Julius Caesar landed in Britain, he did not stay long, returning to Gaul to deal with the rebellion. And when that had been quelled, Caesar went south, across the Rubicon, to defeat Pompey and make himself master of

Rome. So for some time the Romans did not worry about Britain after that first, short invasion.

After Caesar, his nephew Octavius became ruler under the title Caesar Augustus (it was at the time of Caesar Augustus that Christ was born). Under Caesar Augustus and later under Tiberius, Britain was left in peace, mainly because the Romans had enough trouble fighting Germanic tribes across the Rhine. But then came Claudius (the father of Nero), and in his time Roman generals looked around for new conquests. They led their legions across the Channel, nearly a hundred years after Caesar's first invasion.

Some of the Celtic tribes on the coast thought it better to surrender to the Romans without a fight, saving their lives and homes. Many were quite willing to help the Romans against other tribes with whom they had old scores to settle.

However, there was one Celtic king, Caractacus, who was not willing to bow to the Romans. He called upon his people to fight and in a fierce battle he showed the Romans that the Britons were prepared to defend their freedom. But in the end Caractacus was defeated, taken prisoner and thousands of Britons died in the battle.

He was taken to Rome in chains where there was a great triumph and Caractacus was marched through the streets while the Roman crowds jeered and shouted abuse at him. After the triumph he was brought before the Emperor Claudius who said to him: "Barbarian, who comes from a land where people live in huts, have you seen the splendour of our buildings? Have they given you some idea of the wealth and power of Rome?"

And Caractacus answered: "Yes, I have seen it all. But I wonder that people who are so wealthy that they live in houses built of marble, come to our country to rob us of our poor huts."

"What?" cried Claudius. "How dare you speak to me with such impertinence? Do you know that, at a word from me, you will die?"

"Indeed, I know," said Caractacus, "but I have not feared death when I was a king and free. Why should I fear death now when I am a prisoner in chains?"

Then Claudius looked at him and said, "By Jupiter, you are a brave man and I respect courage."

Turning to the guards and commanded: "Strike off his chains and set him free." Then he said to Caractacus, "I give you your freedom. Return in peace to your homeland."

Caractacus answered: "I respect a noble and generous enemy, Caesar Claudius. I shall return to Britain and I will no longer fight against your legions."

When Caractacus returned to Britain he lived to the end of his days in peace with the Romans, who treated him with great respect. Yet the conquest of Britain went on. Rome's lust for power and conquest could never be satisfied.

# 45. Boadicea

Caractacus was fortunate; he had found a Roman ruler who was – at least on this occasion – noble and generous. But not all Romans were like that, and many Britons learned to their bitter cost that the Romans could not always be trusted.

Among the many Celtic tribes in Britain there was one, the Iceni, who were famous as horse breeders and skilled chariot-eers and riders. They had not been conquered by the Romans because the king of this tribe had from the beginning been a friend of the Romans. He thought that the Romans would be fair with people who had been on their side, and he hoped that his tribe could remain independent.

There came a time when this king fell ill; he became weaker and weaker and knew that he was going to die. The King of the Iceni did not fear death, but he was worried about what would happen to his people when he passed away. After his death his wife would rule the Iceni and the king wanted to make sure that the Romans would leave her in peace.

The Roman general in that part of Britain, Catus, had always been a personal friend of the King; so the King asked General Catus to come to his sick-bed and he said: "I have not much longer to live, but I want to make sure that my wife, the Queen, can rule in peace over my people when I die. Now what I want to do is this: I give half of my kingdom to you, to the Romans, if you promise me that my wife can rule in peace over the other half and you will not interfere."

The Roman general, Catus, faithfully promised that the Queen would have nothing to fear from him. So the King of the Iceni died peacefully, trusting that his Roman friend Catus.

After his death, one half of his kingdom came under Roman rule and the other half was ruled by the widowed queen whose name was Boadicea. Very soon after the death of the king, Catus, the Roman general, sent soldiers to Queen Boadicea to demand that she pay tribute and taxes. Queen Boadicea proudly refused, but the soldiers said: "If you barbarians don't pay willingly, we shall make you pay!" And they went and took herds of horses and cattle from the Iceni and drove them away.

Queen Boadicea could not believe that a Roman general would break a promise given to a dying man. She and her two daughters set out to see General Catus at the Roman fort Verulanium (just north of London) where he had his residence. And when she came before Catus she reminded him of his promise. But Catus only laughed at her and said: "If you are not careful I will not only take taxes but your whole kingdom from you." Boadicea answered: "It is you who should be careful not to make an enemy of me, the Queen of a proud and brave people."

This made General Catus very angry. He shouted: "What? You dare to threaten me?"

He called his soldiers and at his command the soldiers beat Queen Boadicea and her daughters with the shafts of the spears. When the poor women were badly bruised and hurt they dragged them roughly to the gates of the town and pushed them out.

Boadicea and her two daughters stumbled on until they reached their own people, the Iceni. And when the Iceni saw how shamefully their queen and her daughters had been treated, a wild roar of rage went up and they swore to revenge the insult.

Other Celtic tribes too had suffered under the harshness, greed and cruelty of the Romans, and they joined forces with the Iceni. Soon a great army of ferocious Celtic warriors was gathered. This army was not led by a man, but by a woman, Queen Boadicea.

Like a raging torrent the Celtic army fell upon the Romans, who were taken by surprise. The Britons stormed the fortress of Verulanium where Catus had his headquarters and the treacherous general was killed in the fighting.

At the time the Commander-in-Chief of all the Roman legions in Britain, Paulinus, was in Wales, fighting the fierce Welsh tribes with a great Roman army. When news of the uprising of the Britons reached him, he and his legions immediately left Wales and marched back to England, where in the meantime Boadicea and her warriors had even stormed the city of Londinium (London).

The two armies, the Romans under Paulinus, and the Britons under Boadicea clashed in a furious battle; the Britons threw themselves again and again with wild shouts against the closed ranks of the Romans. But the Romans stood, shield by shield, unbroken, and when the Britons had exhausted themselves, the legions went into the attack, and at the end of the day the Britons, having lost thousands, gave way and fled. Rome had scored another victory.

Queen Boadicea and her two daughters escaped from the battlefield and reached a forest. Here the Queen stopped and spoke to her daughters. She said: "My children, sooner or later the soldiers of Rome will find us – and if they do we shall be marched in chains through the streets of Rome, and then we shall be strangled in a Roman prison. It is far better to die here, in the green forest on our own soil, than to die in a foreign land, in a dark dungeon by the hand of cruel gaolers."

And she and her daughters took a poison she had carried with her and they died together.

Today in London you can still see a statue of Queen Boadicea. She is shown driving a chariot with two prancing horses. It is a monument in honour of a brave and noble woman.

Queen Boadicea was the last to resist the power of Rome. After her defeat the Romans extended their possessions step by step, reaching further and further North. When a tribe surrendered the Romans treated the people more or less fairly except for the priests, the Druids. Everywhere the Druids were killed without mercy. In Anglesey in Wales there was a great centre of Druid learning – you might say it was both a holy temple and a university for Druids. The Romans killed every person they found there, hundreds of Druids, and destroyed the whole place.

Without the Druids, the Britons soon took up Roman customs, worshipping Roman gods, building houses like the Romans had, wearing togas like the Romans; some even gave up

their own language and spoke Latin. The wealthy Britons even
sent their sons to Rome to be educated there. Within a hundred
years Britain, from the Channel to the Tyne and Solway became
thoroughly Romanised.

In AD 130 the Emperor Hadrian ordered a great stone wall to
be built from east to west which ran from the mouth of the Tyne
to the Solway Firth. Remnants of Hadrian's Wall can still be
seen.

The land north of the wall, Northumberland and Scotland,
was so wild that for a time the Romans left it alone. In the forests and hills of that wild land lived the fierce tribes of the Picts
and Scots who from time to time attacked the wall. Though
later (AD 143) the Romans pushed further north, and even built
an earth wall between the Firth of Forth and the River Clyde
(the Antonine Wall), they never really conquered these tribes,
who took no part in the Roman civilisation in the rest of Britain.

# 46. Alban

Verulanium was the fort where the treacherous General Catus had his residence, where he insulted Queen Boadicea and where he later paid with his life for the insult. But a hundred years later Verulanium, which is about thirty miles north of Londinium (London), showed no trace of warfare between Britons and Romans. Then the town of Verulanium was a little copy of great Rome, with a Forum, with Roman temples, with public baths where you could choose between pools of hot, tepid or cold water. The citizens of Verulanium looked like their ancestors, but their language was Latin, and they wore their togas with the same pride as any citizen of Rome itself.

And if in Rome there was a new fashion in ladies' hairstyles, it did not take long before this fashion was also adopted by the ladies of Verulanium. It was not only fashions which spread from Rome to Britain and all other parts of the Roman Empire, but other things, too. The Governor of Verulanium was worried for he had heard rumours of a dangerous new religion. He had heard of wicked people who called themselves Christian and who worshipped a criminal who had been crucified at the time of Emperor Tiberius. The Governor of Verulanium had not paid much attention to these rumours: surely this wicked new religion would be wiped out in Rome and never get any further. But now it seemed, that – in spite of harsh punishments – this new thing was spreading; it had come to Britain and there were Christians even in Verulanium.

"I will certainly not tolerate this sort of thing in my city of Verulanium," thought the Governor. And he gave his soldiers orders to search every house in Verulanium for Christians, and anybody who admitted that he was a Christian was to be executed. This, thought the Governor, would put an end to this dangerous new religion.

At that time a young Briton named Alban lived in Verulanium. He was from a noble family, had been educated in Rome, and even the Governor of Verulanium treated him with respect. Alban had been brought up to worship Roman gods and had never concerned himself with that new religion which, he thought, must be evil as there was a law against it.

One evening this young man, Alban, was coming home from a visit to a friend. As he approached his house he saw an old man, wrapped in a dark, coarse cloak, huddled at the door. Alban was a kind-hearted, generous person; he felt it was his duty to give food and shelter to poor people. So he spoke to the old man and invited him to come into the house.

"I don't think I should enter your house," said the old man. "It is dangerous to give shelter to me, for I am a Christian and the Governor's soldiers are searching for me." But Alban saw the frail figure, the haggard features of the old man, it was quite clear that he had been without food for days, and Alban felt he could not turn this old man away. He insisted that he had to come into the house, where he was given food and drink and a place to rest his weary body.

The next day Alban talked to the old man and said: "You call yourself a Christian. I have heard the word before and I want you to tell me what it means."

So the old man told him about the Lord Jesus – about His life, death and resurrection. As he listened, Alban felt strangely moved, his whole heart told him that this was the truth. He said to the old man: "I too now believe in Him of whom you have told me, I want to become a Christian."

And the old man thanked God for having led him to this house and he blessed Alban and baptised him. They were still talking when there was a loud knock on the door. A servant rushed into the room where Alban and his visitor were, and told Alban that the Governor's soldiers were outside wanting to search the house for an old man had been seen the in this part of the town wearing an old, rough cloak.

"Quick," cried Alban, "take my cloak and leave by the back door!"

The old man protested, he said: "If I flee, your life is in danger."

But Alban said: "Your task is to teach others as you have taught me. Leave me and let me serve the Lord Jesus in my way."

The old man blessed him, took Alban's cloak and left safely by the back door. Alban took the worn, ragged cloak which the old man had left behind and wrapped himself in it. A moment later the Governor's soldiers burst in, saw a hooded figure in the old cloak kneeling in prayer and seized him and took him away.

Alban spent the night in prison. The next morning he was brought before the Governor who recognised him and was very angry that, by this ruse, Alban had helped the old man to escape. He shouted: "How can you, a man of noble family, a man educated in Rome, help a criminal to escape?"

Alban answered: "He was not a criminal, he was a servant of Christ, and so am I."

"You, a Christian?" cried the Governor. "You must be mad. I give you one more chance. I will spare your life if you offer a sacrifice to our gods."

"No," answered Alban. "A Christian does not offer sacrifices to the gods of Rome."

"Take him away," shouted the Governor, "and put him to death!"

An officer and some soldiers took him away and and led him through the streets of Verulanium and out of the city gates. There, outside the city, he was told to kneel down. Then the officer told one of the soldiers to take his sword and cut Alban's head off. But the soldier hesitated.

"What is the matter with you?" cried the officer, "have you not heard my order?"

"I have heard you," said the soldier, "but I cannot kill this man. I have known him for many years and I know he is a good man and not a criminal."

"Then you will die with him!" shouted the officer, and he drew his sword and struck the soldier down before beheading Alban.

In spite of these cruel persecutions, Christianity grew and spread in Britain as in Rome, and the Christians always remembered the names of the martyrs, the men and women who died for their faith. Many centuries later a church was built on the place where Alban had given his life for his faith. It became a great abbey and the town of Verulanium is now called St Albans.

# 47. The Germanic Tribes

The last Roman Emperor we heard about was Nero, a man who was both evil and mad. He set Rome on fire and when the people of Rome cursed him he blamed the Christians for the fire, which led to the terrible persecutions. In the end the legions revolted against Nero and he died by his own hand. After Nero came emperors who were much more like Augustus, hard but clever men who saw to it that there was justice and order in all the lands under Roman rule. Of course they still persecuted the Christians, for the Roman lust for power could not tolerate a religion which called all human beings brothers.

But otherwise, these Emperors ruled wisely and under one of them, Hadrian, Rome reached the height of its power. Just imagine the Empire which stretched from Hadrian's Wall in the North of England to the River Nile in Egypt and the whole coast of North Africa. It stretched from Spain in the West to the River Euphrates in the East. Roman forts and Roman legions stood guard along the River Rhine and the River Danube. It was a mighty empire and from every corner of this empire taxes and tributes flowed to the centre, to Rome.

Just outside Rome is the Villa of Hadrian, but it was not merely a villa. It was a little town: there were two theatres, several libraries, several baths, quite apart from living quarters for Hadrian, his court and his slaves, as well as stables for horses and chariots. There were also enormous gardens with large ponds and even a hippodrome for horse-races. Today there are only ruins left. It is a strange feeling to stand by these enormous walls and arches and to think that they were built for a man whose power reached from Scotland's hills to the deserts of Africa.

Thousands of cities and towns flourished in that great empire. They were connected by the straight roads where

Roman legions marched, where goods of every description travelled on horse-drawn carts, where travellers could journey in safety from one part of the Empire to the other. On these roads there also travelled the men and women who carried the message of Christ with them. And no matter how many Christians were caught and executed, all over the Roman Empire there were souls ready to receive the message: slaves and noblemen, soldiers and traders, men and women. And no emperor and no persecution could stop it.

Under the Emperor Hadrian, Rome reached the peak of its power, but this peak did not last long. Beneath Hadrian's successes Roman power was beginning to crumble, first slowly, then faster and faster. What was it that made the Roman Empire crumble away? It was the coming of a new people from the north-east, the Germanic tribes.

The original home of the Germanic people had been Siberia. In our time Siberia is a very cold land, only few people living there. But about four thousand or five thousand years ago Siberia had a warmer climate, and was a land of wide, grass-covered plains. And the Germanic tribes lived in these plains as nomads. Riding horses and herding cattle, they moved with their herds from one grazing place to another.

When the climate of Siberia became colder, the Germanic tribes began to move westwards. Slowly, over many generations, they drifted across Russia until they reached Scandinavia, the countries which are now called Norway and Sweden. The Scandinavian peninsula at that time (about 2500 years ago) had a much warmer climate than it has now. And so, for a time, the Germanic tribes settled in Scandinavia, it became their home in Europe.

But the Scandinavian climate also changed: the winters became colder and longer, there was no longer enough grazing for all the herds of cattle, and some of the Germanic tribes now moved south, they moved into the lands which we now call Germany. There were already people there, Celtic people who had come from around Persia and settled in the central parts of Europe long before. But the Germanic tribes fought the Celts and conquered them and moved further south until they reached the Alps where they stopped for a time.

Remember the Cimbri and Teutons who came sledding down the Alps into Italy and burnt the Roman cities until Marius defeated them. These Cimbri and Teutons were only a tiny wave that had spilled over into Italy. For a time no other waves came across.

Some Germanic tribes turned West – they crossed the River Rhine and invaded Gaul. This gave Julius Caesar the excuse to march his legions into Gaul to help the Gauls against the Germanic invaders. Not only did he drive the Germanic tribes back across the Rhine, but he conquered Gaul for Rome.

From the time of Caesar onwards, there was always fighting between the Germanic tribes and the Roman legions. As a great tide sends wave after wave against a dam, so one tribe and then another and another attacked Roman forts, Roman settlements across the Rhine and across the Danube. No matter how often they were beaten back, they soon came again.

But the Romans had changed; as masters of a great empire they had become too fond of comfort, of luxury, of pleasure, and they no longer enjoyed fighting. But they were clever and thought: "We shall make these barbarians fight our battles for us."

They sent their messengers to some of these Germanic tribes and the messengers said: "What you people really want is land where you can settle. We Romans have plenty of land, and we are willing to give you land in Gaul. In return your men must be willing to fight for us and keep other invading tribes out."

The tribes who received such offers agreed. Within a short time, the Roman armies had only Roman generals and, perhaps, a few Roman officers, while the soldiers were mostly Germanic people, besides a few legions of Gauls and Britons. And these foreign troops protected Roman frontiers and kept the other Germanic tribes out, at least for a time. But this clever Roman ploy could not work forever. Once the Romans were no longer prepared to fight their own battles, the days of Roman power were numbered.

# 48. The Empire Divided

These Germanic tribes used to live a nomadic life in the grasslands of Siberia. Nomads move from place to place with their herds and do not sow or harvest. They let the flocks and herds graze as long as there is grass in one place, and then they move on to the next place. A nomad's occupation was only hunting, looking after his animals, or fighting, but he would not till the soil.

Later when the Germanic tribes came to Europe, they could not roam as freely as in Asia, they settled and farmed the land for their food. By then they had conquered the Celtic peoples, who became their servants or serfs, as they were called, and these serfs worked the land for their masters.

But the free-men, the warriors, would not do any work. They considered fighting and hunting as the only two things worth doing. And they loved fighting. It was shameful for a man to die of old age in his bed. They called it straw-death, for their beds were pallets of straw. They said that if a man died this shameful death on a straw-bed, his soul would go down to the dark underworld where the goddess Hel ruled.

The only death for a man was to die fighting in battle. Then from Valhalla, from the castle of the gods, fully armed maidens came, riding white horses. These armed maidens, called Valkyries, carried the soul of the warrior up to Valhalla, to the gods. But this happened only to those who died fighting, not to those who died in their beds. And when the soul was in Valhalla, this was by no means the end of all fighting. Every day all the heroes and warriors in Valhalla went out to a great field – and there they fought and battled with each other, but when the fight was over all the wounds healed and all the dead came to life again and so they could fight again the next day. For these

Germanic tribes even heaven was a place where they could go on fighting forever.

Not only their religion but all their stories and songs were about wars and fighting. When the men sat together at a banquet, they enjoyed listening to singers who recited long poems of battles and wars and heroes. When these people did not fight they wanted to hear about fighting.

They worshipped the gods Odin, also called Wotan (Wednesday comes from Wotan's day), Thor (Thursday), Tiw or Ziu, the war-god (Tuesday), Fria, the goddess of love (Friday). We still have the names of their gods in the names of the days of the week.

But like the Celts, the Germanic tribes did not worship their gods in temples, or in any building made by human hands. They worshipped them in the open, in a glade of a forest, or on the top of a high hill. When a refreshing cool wind blew on the mountain-top, they said: "Can you feel how this fresh wind makes you strong, vigorous and healthy? That is the power of Wotan in the wind." And when thunder rolled and lightning flashed they said: "This is Thor flinging his hammer that always flies back into his hand." They saw their gods everywhere in nature.

They were tall and strong people, and in many ways the Germanic people looked like the Celts. But in other ways they were quite different. The Celtic people were ever ready to talk – and they specially liked to boast of their deeds. The Germanic people did not boast and they talked but little. The Celtic people had a vivid imagination and liked beautiful things, and even the men among the Celts liked to wear colourful clothes. The Germanic people were much more practical, they were not fond of ornaments and dressed in coarse woollen cloth.

As every boy was expected to become a warrior, the Germanic people could see no purpose in bringing up a weakly looking baby boy: so every newborn boy was laid at the father's feet and if the father decided that this baby was not likely to become a strong, healthy man, it was taken out to a mountain-side and left to die. This was not done out of cruelty, but because these people who

loved fighting above all things thought that a weakling who could
not fight for himself would not have a life worth living.

These were the people who threatened the Roman
Empire. If all the Germanic tribes had united, Rome would
have been conquered by them much sooner. But as it was,
each tribe chose its own time to wage war against Rome.
Some tribes would rather fight each other, and other tribes
helped the Romans fighting as soldiers against other
Germanic tribes. And so the Roman Empire lasted longer
than it would have done if the Germanic tribes had all united
against Rome.

But these foreign barbarians who had become Roman soldiers, did not feel about Rome as a true Roman would have
felt. And if a general called his legions together and said, "I
want to become Emperor. If you fight for me, I promise you
rich rewards," these foreign soldiers would cheer, march to
Rome and kill whoever was Emperor, and then put their own
general in his place. But after a few years or even months
another general would do the same thing: with the help of
the barbarians he killed the man who was now Emperor and
took his place.

Under these conditions there was little law or order in the
Roman Empire, the legions fought each other more than they
fought invaders, on the frontiers the Germanic tribes raided and
plundered as much as they pleased and even Italy was no longer
safe from invaders.

At last, after fifty years of this disorder and chaos there was
an Emperor who was a ruthless and hard man. But he established peace and order and drove the invaders out. The name of
this Emperor was Diocletian. He realised that it was too difficult for one man to rule the great Roman Empire, keep the
barbarians out, and see that the legions did not start again set-
ting up their own Emperor. So he decided to divide the Roman
Empire into two parts, the Western Empire (which included
Italy, Gaul, Spain, Britain) and the Eastern Empire (Greece,
Syria, Egypt).

Diocletian himself ruled the Eastern Empire, and his friend
Maximianus ruled the Western Empire. As long as these two

lived, the system worked well. (Octavius and Mark Antony had once made a similar division).

But both Diocletian and Maximianus were sworn enemies of Christianity, and in their time the worst persecutions of the Christians took place with thousands being killed. But this was also the last persecution, for after Diocletian everything changed for the Christians.

# 49. The Vision of Constantine

Diocletian, the Emperor who divided the Roman Empire in two parts, had no son. But when he grew old he wanted to retire and to hand the crown and the burden of ruling to a younger man. He chose as his successor a Roman nobleman called Constantine.

Constantine was born in Britain, in York; his father had been Governor of Britain and his mother was a British princess. As successor of Diocletian, Constantine became ruler of the Eastern Empire. Soon afterwards Maximianus, the ruler of the West, died and was followed by his son, Maxentius. He hated the Christians as much as his father had done. But Constantine was different. His mother, Helena, the British princess, was a pagan but also believed that Christ was a great and powerful being. She worshipped Christ as well as the Roman gods. So Constantine, although he was a pagan, did not hate the Christians, for his own mother had also worshipped Christ.

But this was not the only difference between Constantine, Emperor of the East and Maxentius, Emperor of the West. They did not trust each other, they were jealous of each other's power, and in the end they decided that only one of them was fit to rule. It was always the same in Roman history, from Romulus and Remus, to Caesar and Pompey, and to Octavius and Mark Antony: they could not share power. And so it came to war between Maxentius and Constantine.

Maxentius had gathered an army of two hundred thousand men which he kept in Rome. He waited for Constantine to attack him. Constantine had only half that number. As he marched his army into Italy, Constantine was worried and began to doubt whether he could defeat his enemy. One evening Constantine was riding at the head of his army when he looked up into the sky and saw a strange vision. He saw rays of light which formed a great shining cross in the sky and above the cross appeared in shining letters the words: *In hoc signo vinces,* which means: "In this sign you shall be victorious." Then the vision disappeared, it grew dark and night fell. The soldiers set up a camp and Constantine lay down to rest in his camp.

For a long time he could not find sleep, he wondered about the vision he had seen and what it could mean. At long last he fell asleep – and in his sleep there came a wonderful dream. In the dream he saw Jesus Christ who spoke to him and said: "The sign you have seen in the sky is the sign that will give you victory over your enemy. If your soldiers carry my name into the battle the enemies will be scattered."

When he awoke next morning Constantine no longer had any doubt what he should do. He gave orders that a flag should be made painted with the first two Greek letters of the word "Christ." **XP**. And the flagstaff was to be in the shape of a cross, but made of gold.

Now most of Constantine's soldiers were already Christian, and when they saw that their leader, Constantine, gave them a flag with the initials of Christ on it, they cheered loudly and painted the sign of the cross on their shields. The cross – the instrument by which only the worst criminals were executed in ancient Rome – had become the sign under which these soldiers now proudly and confidently marched against the pagan enemy.

In the meantime Maxentius, the Emperor in Rome, had turned for advice to his gods, the pagan gods. At the time of Tarquinius a sibyl had come and had sold him three books which had been kept in the Temple of Jupiter on the Capitoline Hill. Whenever there was any danger for Rome, the priests had consulted the books of the sibyl to find if there was any advice about what should be done.

If Maxentius, with his two hundred thousand men, had stayed inside the strong, thick walls which protected Rome, Constantine could never have taken the city with only half that number of soldiers. But Maxentius asked the priests to look into the books of the sibyl and find out what he should do. The priests studied the books and then told Maxentius that he should march his soldiers out of the city to meet Constantine in open battle – he should attack Constantine, not merely fight him off from the walls. Maxentius took this advice.

When Constantine and his army reached the plains outside Rome, they expected to have the terrible task of storming the mighty walls, but to their surprise the gates in the walls opened, a great drawbridge was let down over the deep, wide moat and over the bridge Maxentius himself led his soldiers.

In the battle which ensued, Constantine's legionaries fought like lions, it seemed as if they had strength and courage that was more than human, each soldier was more than a match for two of Maxentius' men. Terrified by the furious onslaught, Maxentius' soldiers turned and ran back to the drawbridge, Maxentius fleeing with them. But when he was just on the bridge with hundreds of soldiers pressing around him, the bridge broke under the great weight of men. Maxentius and all those around him fell into the water-filled moat and drowned.

Without their leader, the remainder of the army threw away their weapons and surrendered. The battle was over, and Constantine marched as victor into Rome. This battle, which changed the whole course of history, took place on October 28, 312. Some three hundred years after the birth of Christ this battle, fought under the sign of the cross, brought victory to the Christians.

In the following year Constantine passed a law throughout the Empire that all Christians could follow their religion and worship Christ unhindered and in freedom. He did more than that: he favoured Christians and no one could hold a high position unless he was a Christian. Now the Christian religion spread rapidly, and, in time, the pagan religion – the worship of Jupiter, Apollo, Venus – disappeared. Many of the ancient temples were converted into churches, or demolished and churches built in their place. After three hundred years of persecution, the Christian religion had now risen from the catacombs and triumphed over the persecutors.

But the people of Rome did not like Constantine – they had been on Maxentius' side, and Constantine had no liking for Rome or its people. He decided to find himself a new capital, further away from the Germanic tribes in the North. Constantine thought that Roman history had begun with Aeneas who had come from the East, from Troy. He wanted his new capital somewhere near the site of Troy. He went to Byzantium, a city on the Hellespont, on the straits between the Mediterranean and the Black Sea. He renamed this splendid place City of Constantine, which in Greek is Constantinopolis *(polis* is city), and we call Constantinople (now it is called Istanbul).

So, proud Rome was no longer the centre of the Empire, the centre was Constantinople. It was a wise decision, for soon the time would come when the invading tribes from the North could no longer be kept out of Italy.

# 50. The Monks

Constantine had brought about an enormous change. Christians were no longer persecuted, and no longer lived in fear of their lives. Not only were they free to worship in their own way, it was even an advantage to be a Christian. The Emperors themselves were Christian and if anyone wanted a favour – a high position or a career – he had to be a Christian. No wonder that the number of Christians now grew rapidly while the number of pagans declined.

Christians no longer met in the Catacombs, but now wanted churches. Many pagan temples were only visited by a few people, so the Christians often took over the temples, banished the pagans and pagan priests, threw out the statues of Roman gods, and turned the temples into churches. In some parts of the Roman Empire they turned against the pagans and attacked them. In Egypt a wise, good woman Hypathia was killed by a mob of so-called Christians only because she was a pagan.

And the Christians also quarrelled among themselves. Their disputes about their religion and what they should believe often ended in fighting. The leaders of the Christian priests, the bishops, came together to lay down rules about what was right and what was wrong to believe, but then other bishops did not accept these rules.

There was also another change: in the days when Christians had lived in fear of their lives, when any day could bring a cruel death to them, they had lived very simply without much thought of luxury, comforts or amusements. But now, when the Emperors themselves were Christian, when the highest and best paid positions were given to Christians, they enjoyed wealth, power and luxury just as much as the pagans had done. Many had only become Christian because it brought advantages, but they had no wish to change their way of life; they had just as many slaves and just as much luxury as before.

But not all people thought in this way. There were some who remembered that Christ had lived in poverty; they thought that if you love money, luxury, pleasures too much then you cannot love God as much as He should be loved, for Christ had said: "Love God above all." The people who thought like that, turned away from a life of amusements, comforts, possessions and slaves.

Remember in ancient India the hermits went into the forest where they ate very little, fasted, and spent their time in prayer. Something similar happened among the Christians. Some men withdrew from all the earthly pleasures. and became hermits. But now, in Christian times these hermits were called "monks," from the Greek *monachos*, "one who lives alone." The other Christians, those who liked their pleasures and comforts and were quite unable to give them up (they were of course, the majority) had a great respect for the monks. They called them holy men or men of God. They thought God Himself would reward them if they gave such a monk the little food or drink he needed.

One of the first men who took up the life as a monk was called Antony who lived in Egypt *(c.* AD 250–356). Antony could not withdraw into the forest as the hermits of ancient India had done, for Egypt had no forests; he went into the desert where he lived in a cave in a rock. The nearest human habitation, a little village, was two or three hours' walk away, but the people of that village, knowing that a holy man had come to live near them, came from time to time and left a little food and a jug of water at the cave.

Antony lived in the desert by himself. There were many days when he had to go without food or drink, but he was glad of it, for he felt that as his body grew weaker with hunger, his soul grew stronger in prayer and worship. Even when the people had brought some food to him, he made himself fast and go for another day or two without touching the bread or the water.

Strange things happened to him in these days when he sat in the scorching sun of the desert, trying to forget the pangs of hunger and thirst which racked his body by concentrating his mind on prayer. It was like a contest between mind and body, the mind saying: "I am immortal spirit, I am stronger than the body, I can forget the hunger of the body if I turn all my thoughts to God," and the body saying: "I want food, I want drink."

But for a monk like Antony, this contest between mind and body, this battle between mind and body, was the reason for which he had withdrawn into the desert, for only in such a contest could he discover that the mind was stronger than the body, that mind and soul can triumph over the body.

As Antony was fighting this battle, this contest between mind and body, in the heat of the desert, there appeared to him a beautiful woman holding out a bowl of juicy sweet oranges, figs and other fruit. But Antony cried out: "You are only an evil spirit, a devil come to tempt me, go away, I want nothing of your accursed gifts!"

As soon as he had said so, the woman changed her shape, becoming a horrible monster with horns and claws, and other monsters appeared beside her, and the whole horde of demons attacked Antony and he felt as if they were tearing him to pieces. But with his last strength Antony cried: "In the name of the Father, the Son and the Holy Ghost, go from me!" And, with one stroke they all disappeared and Antony found himself lying on the hot sand of the desert under the scorching sun.

When the people of the nearest village came the next time with food, Antony told them what had happened to him, and they regarded him with even greater awe and respect than ever before. It may sound strange to us, but when the story of Antony spread, quite a number of people were attracted by such a kind of life and became hermits in the desert.

Two hundred years after Antony all over the Roman Empire there were many monks – perhaps a few thousand – in the desert, but in forests or on hills and mountains. One such monk from Italy, Benedict, thought that this lonely monk's life in deserts or forests was not of much help to other people. He felt it would be better and more Christian if the monks did something for other people in the world. To do anything useful they would have to live together in groups, as some already did.

Under Benedict's leadership the monks changed their way of life. They lived together in communities, or brotherhoods as they were called. And each brotherhood had a leader whom it had to obey, the abbot. Each community built a house for itself called a monastery. There the monks still fasted and prayed, but they also worked tending gardens and orchards, copying holy books (for printing had not yet been invented), teaching children of the poor, for there were no schools and only rich people had private tutors for their sons. And even more important was that the monks went among the Germanic tribes to convert them to the Christian faith. Through Benedict the monks became people who lived in self-chosen poverty, but did many important things for others. A time was coming when the monasteries would be the only places of civilisation, of knowledge and of human kindness. For the Roman Empire and all its civilisation was crumbling and breaking under the onslaught of the barbarians. It is owing to Benedict, the founder of the monasteries, that anything of Roman civilisation survived at all after the collapse of the Roman Empire.

A monk wore only one garment – a sack-like long robe made from a coarse, heavy cloth and held together in the middle with a rope. At the back was a cowl (hood). To become a monk you had to make three vows: the vow of poverty, that you would never own anything; the vow of chastity, that you would never marry, for with a wife and family you could not wholeheartedly serve the community of monks; and the vow of obedience, that you would undertake any work however hard, unpleasant or dangerous, at the command of the abbot, and not just follow you own whim.

It was a sacrifice to become a monk, but the men who became monks felt that only in such a life of self-sacrifice could they serve God in the right way. And in the terrible times which came, such men were needed.

# 51. Attila the Hun

In the vast grassland plains of Siberia, where the Germanic peoples had come from, lived another people, the Huns. They were nomads who roamed the plains on small but strong, shaggy ponies. And the horses were more important to the Huns than anything else. They not only fought and hunted on horseback, but often lived for weeks and months, eating, drinking and even sleeping in the saddle.

Their tents and their clothes were made of horse-skin. From mare's milk they made an intoxicating drink, a potent concoction that could make them drunk. Their main food was horse-meat, but they rarely cooked the meat, usually just putting a chunk of horse-meat under their saddle and riding on it until it was soft enough to be eaten.

When the Huns went to war they showed no mercy. Old people and young children who were no use as slaves were killed; houses and anything else they could not carry away were burnt down. Wherever they went they left a trail of destruction and corpses.

To the East of Siberia there was the great, flourishing Empire of China. For several centuries the Huns made raids into China, devastating fields, burning down villages, robbing and plundering. But in about 220 BC the Chinese Emperor made an end to these raids, building a high and broad wall all along the borders of China, with watchtowers every few miles. The wall ran for hundreds of miles, and day and night Chinese soldiers patrolled these walls. Whenever the Huns came they were driven back. The Great Wall of China put a stop to the raids of the Huns. They could no longer rob and plunder in the East, and so they turned West.

Over the following centuries the Huns left the wild lands of Siberia migrating west towards Europe. When on the move, it was like a flood of ferocious horsemen; anything that stood in the way of this flood was smashed, burnt, killed and destroyed. They traversed the land which is now called Russia and came to the part of Europe which has ever since been called Hungary, the land of the Huns. At that time it was an empty land, the people who now live in Hungary came much later. For a while the Huns settled in Hungary. They were divided into many tribes and each tribe had its own king, but one king made himself leader of all tribes.

Attila, the great king of all Huns, was ferocious – he had great plans, great ambitions and an iron will. One day a herdsman brought Attila an old sword he had found under a stone. Attila cried out: "This is the Sword that the gods have sent me that I may conquer the world."

And under Attila's leadership the Huns left Hungary and swept into Western Europe like a swarm of locusts, and fear and terror went before them.

The Germanic warriors whom they encountered first were struck with horror at the sight of these hordes. They seemed like demons from hell let loose on the world. Even the bravest of the Germanic warriors turned and fled. Villages and towns went up in flames, fields were laid waste, people were slaughtered and all over Europe the cry went up: "The Huns have been sent as a punishment for our sins. They are the whip or the scourge by which God punishes us. Attila is the scourge of God."

And so Attila and his Huns reached Gaul where the Romans and Germanic tribes had been fighting each other for a long time. Now, before this terrible enemy, they joined forces and defeated Attila in a great battle at Chalons in 451. Driven from Gaul, Attila still had a big army which now turned south and stormed into Italy. The Roman armies scattered before the Huns, northern Italy was turned into ruins, and the Huns made for Rome. There was no longer an army which could defend Rome against these wild invaders.

In their despair, the people of Rome turned to one man who should plead with Attila and beg of him to spare the city and its inhabitants. The people of Rome were all Christian and the man to whom they turned was the Bishop of Rome, Leo. He was a very old man, but he went alone to see Attila.

The King of the Huns looked down on Bishop Leo from his horse and smiled grimly. He had never spared a life or a city, why should he spare Rome and miss the rich plunder which he and his Huns would find there?

But the old bishop said to him: "I have come to warn you Attila. The spirits of St Peter and St Paul who died for Christ in this city of Rome stand before God, and their curse will be upon you, if you destroy Rome."

Attila was thoughtful. Perhaps these spirits were really powerful, perhaps their curse was something to fear. And as he thought, he looked up into the sky and it seemed to him that he saw angels with glittering swords guarding Rome. It was better not to challenge these beings. "Go back, old man," said Attila, "I will not touch your city, we have already treasure enough."

Bishop Leo returned with the joyful news to Rome. That same night a sickness, an epidemic, broke out among the Huns, hundreds of them died, and Attila hastened away with his men. It was better to get out of this place and not to rouse the wrath of these strange gods or spirits.

They returned to Hungary, laden with the treasures they had taken from hundreds of cities. Now Attila thought it was time to increase his power by marrying Hildegunde, the daughter of a great Germanic King. Her father could not dare to refuse the mighty king of the Huns. Poor Hildegunde nearly fainted when she was brought to Attila and saw her bridegroom for the first time. But a great wedding-feast was held, where the Huns drank until they fell senseless to the ground. At last the feast was over, and Attila was alone with his bride. He took her in his arms to kiss her, but in her dress Hildegunde had hidden a dagger which she drew and plunged into his heart. So Attila, the Scourge of God, died. In the darkness of night, Hildegunde fled and escaped to her father.

When the Huns found Attila dead in the morning, they wailed and cried with sorrow. Slaves buried him with all his treasures, then they were killed so that no one should ever know where the treasure was. Then the Huns broke up. Some offered their services as soldiers to the Romans, some joined the Germanic tribes, some went back to Asia. So the Huns disappeared as suddenly as they had come.

But the fear they had instilled lasted for generations and the Germanic tribes which had fled the Huns were now all on the move, the great migration of peoples, at it is called, had begun.

# 52. The Fall of Rome

The Huns, the Scourge of God, had disappeared, but their coming had brought enormous changes, for now all the Germanic tribes had been unsettled; some tribes had left their homesteads in the heart of Europe and had fled before the Huns reached them, some had joined forces with the Huns and moved with them across Europe, other tribes had joined forces with the Romans against the common foe. All these tribes were no longer settled anywhere – by the time the Huns disappeared, all the Germanic tribes were on the move. They moved in all directions: towards the West into Gaul, towards the South into the Italian Peninsula and the Balkan Peninsula.

Just imagine these many tribes – each having a few thousand people – on the move: their possessions and the small children piled on big, horse-drawn covered carts, the men wearing eagle-winged helmets, armed with spears, battle-axes and swords, riding beside the carts, the women driving herds of cattle along. Such a column, miles long, consisting of carts, herds, people, horses, straggled along in a cloud of dust. Ahead of the column rode the scouts; if they reported that Roman troops, a Roman fort or people of another tribe were in the neighbourhood, the whole column quickly changed into battle-formation: the warriors forming a circle with the carts and herds, the women and children in the middle.

The Roman soldiers who were sent to stop these roving tribes from entering Roman dominions were themselves no longer Roman, they were often Germanic people who had been given land by the Romans to make them allies of Rome. But even if these defenders beat back one of these tribes, soon another and another appeared. There was no end to it; it was a tide that could not be held off for long. In the history books this great tide of Germanic tribes on the move is called the migration of peoples.

One of these tribes, the largest and most warlike, was the Goths. In Sweden today there is the city of Göteborg, "Castle of the Goths" which used to be the home of the Goths. But they had long since left Scandinavia, and moved south through Germany, and were heading for Constantinople. The Roman Emperor in Constantinople, a weak young man, had no wish to make war against the Goths. There was another way of keeping them away: he offered Alaric, the King of the Goths, gold and rich treasures to leave Constantinople in peace, and so the city was saved from being burned and plundered.

The King of the Goths, Alaric, had at one time been soldiering for the Romans. He had been to Rome and seen the wealth and the treasures which, over hundreds of years, had accumulated in Rome. He was therefore quite willing to spare Constantinople, specially as he was well paid in gold for doing so, because there were even greater riches to be found in Rome. So Alaric led his Goths from the Balkans into Italy and to Rome.

At this time the Roman Empire was again been divided between two rulers. The eastern part was ruled by the Emperor in Constantinople who had bribed Alaric. The western Empire was ruled by Honorius in Rome. This western Emperor was even weaker and more foolish than the other one: his only interest in life was breeding beautiful cocks while the real task of ruling was left to a general, Stilicho. The general, however, was not Roman but came from one of the Germanic tribes. The Romans did not like being ruled by a barbarian, no matter how clever and brave he was, and just at the time when Alaric and his Goths poured into Italy, Stilicho, the only man who could have saved Rome, was put to death. The Goths now went unhindered through Italy and came to Rome.

The Emperor, this weak and foolish young man, simply left Rome when the Goths, led by Alaric, were approaching. He went to the city of Ravenna where he had a beautiful villa. There he played with his most precious possession, a cock so beautiful and strong that it was called Rome. That cock called Rome was much more important to the Emperor than the real Rome.

The real Rome, the city of Caesar and Augustus, was now surrounded by the wild Goths. The people of Rome still had their pride: they were ready to fight for their city. However, they thought they could at least try to save their lives and their possessions by talking to the King of the Goths, Alaric. And so two Roman Senators went to Alaric.

It was a strange sight: the two Senators, still wearing the toga of ancient times, pleading with this barbarian king; Rome which had once ruled the world was now begging a barbarian for mercy. But, being Romans, they were still proud and said to Alaric: "There is not a man in Rome who will not fight you from the walls and in the streets, if you try to take Rome by force."

But Alaric laughed and said: "You know, the thicker the grass is, the easier can it be cut."

Then the two Senators said: "Under what conditions would you spare the city?"

"You must hand over all the gold, silver and jewels there are in Rome, whether they belong to the state or to a private person."

The Senators cried out: "But what will you leave us?"

"Your life, nothing else," answered Alaric.

When the Senators brought this sad news back to the city, the Romans were desperate and decided to fight for Rome and not surrender. But among the slaves there were many who came from Germanic tribes, who had been taken prisoner in the endless fighting on the frontiers. These slaves knew that wherever Alaric went, he set Germanic slaves free and so they were looking forward to the coming of the Goths. During the night these Germanic slaves crept to the gates, fell upon the guards at the gates and killed them. Then they opened the gates and the Goths poured in.

So Rome fell to the Goths in AD 410. Mighty Rome, the city that had once ruled the greatest empire in the world was taken by the Goths. Neither Hannibal, nor the first Germanic invaders, the Cimbri and Teutons, had been able to take Rome. But now it fell to the Goths with barely a fight.

It must be said for Alaric that he kept his word: there was

very little killing, only some slaves revenged themselves on cruel masters and killed them. The Goths themselves were satisfied with plundering, with taking all the gold, silver and jewels from every house and every temple. All the treasure that for centuries had come to Rome was now taken from her.

The one person who was least concerned about the fall of Rome, was the Emperor in his villa at Ravenna. When a slave came running, crying out: "Rome is lost!" the Emperor replied: "But I saw him yesterday, he looked quite well," his only thought was for his cock called Rome. And when he was told that it was the city of Rome that was lost, he was quite relieved to hear that his cock was all right.

Having taken what treasures there were in Rome, Alaric had no wish to stay. He wanted to lead his Goths on to Spain and from there to Africa. The Goths left the city and moved south. But they were still in Italy when Alaric fell ill and, within a few days, died. Nearby was a river, the Busento. The Goths first built a channel to divert waters from the river. In the dry river-bed they buried Alaric, and with their great king they buried most of the treasure of Rome. Then they turned the river back into its old bed so that it flowed over Alaric's grave. All the slaves who had done the work were then killed so that they could not pass on the secret where Alaric's treasure was hidden. So it might still be there under the waters of the River Busento in Italy.

Less than fifty years later another Germanic tribe took Rome by force; they were the Vandals who were fiercer and more terrible than the Goths. They plundered and burnt, and killed without mercy. Then they loaded their plunder on ships and sailed away to Africa. To this day people who destroy things for no reason are called "vandals" after this tribe of barbarians who ravaged Rome.

After these two invasions, the Goths and the Vandals, Rome ceased to be a great city. There was still a Roman Empire of the West, but the Emperors of the West used Ravenna as their capital. The Rome of the Caesars had gone, but another Rome was very slowly growing. This new, coming Rome was the seat of the Popes, the centre of the Catholic Church. But at that time, after the invasion of the barbarians, the city was only a shadow of what it had been, and most of its proud buildings were in ruins.

# 53. The End of the Empire

The Roman Empire was falling to pieces: the Huns had ravaged it, the Goths plundered Rome, the Vandals pillaged it, and even the soldiers who still fought for Rome were themselves often Germanic warriors who, for money, adventure, or lust of fighting, defended the tottering, crumbling Empire. Both the Eastern and the Western Empire depended entirely on the mercenaries who fought for them.

Most of the people in the Roman Empire were Christian, and some of the mercenary soldiers had also become Christian. But the Germanic tribes who attacked, wave upon wave, from the forests of Central Europe, were still mostly pagan. But there were men who took on the task of bringing the message of Christ to these Germanic tribes: the monks. The Roman Empire might be tottering and falling, but these missionaries felt that the kingdom of Christ should grow.

It took a stout heart and great courage to go unarmed among these wild tribes who worshipped Odin and Thor, to live among them, and to try and persuade this war-loving people to believe in the God of Love and in Christ. Only a monk – only a man who had no family ties, no possessions to worry about, only a man who was willing to give his life for his faith – could go among these fierce warriors to preach them the religion of mercy and compassion.

These monks knew very well that even if they were successful, and the warriors became Christian, they would not change their way of life immediately. It would take many generations before these warlike people would not only be Christian in name but also in deed. But a beginning was made.

Severin was such a monk. He had chosen to live among the tribes along the River Danube. Where today the city of Vienna lies, Severin lived in a little hut. From a little plot of land he grew the food he needed by hard work. From time to time a warrior or even a nobleman would come to his hut and ask him questions about his God. He might come a second or third time and listen to Severin's stories of Jesus, and, one day, the warrior or the nobleman would say: "I want to become a Christian." And when this happened Severin felt like a general after a great victory, and would thank God for the great joy He had given him.

One day a new visitor came to Severin, a man from the North. He was a warrior so tall that he had to stand bowed in the little hut; he was poorly dressed but there was great strength in his body. The Germanic warrior greeted Severin saying: "My name is Odoacer. I have left my tribe who live by the North Sea and I am on my way to Rome to become a soldier in their legions. I am poor – as you can see from my clothes – but I am strong and my strength will, perhaps, help me to find good fortune as a soldier. I heard of you as a wise and good man; perhaps you can tell me if my hopes are wise or not."

Severin smiled at the tall man and said: "My friend, I can see a time when you will wear the finest garments that can be found. Yet, fine garments are not the only thing that matters." And he began to tell Odoacer of Jesus.

Odoacer was so enthralled by what Severin told him, that he stayed for a time with Severin. When at last he left to seek his fortune in Italy he had become a Christian.

Being tall and strong, he was easily accepted into the legions. He showed great courage in many battles, and became an officer, reaching higher and higher rank. One day he became Commander-in-Chief, the highest officer, of the legions.

Only one man was still above him, the Emperor of the West himself. But at that time the Emperor was only a young boy, called Romulus Augustulus, Romulus after the first king, and Augustulus (little Augustus) after Caesar Augustus. Despite these grand names the Emperor was only a boy of ten and so unable to rule. It was Odoacer who ruled the Western Empire for him.

But then Odoacer began to wonder why he, the barbarian, should bow before a young Roman boy, why his legions who

were nearly all Germanic people like himself, should be the
servants of the Romans who could no longer fight for themselves. What was all this talk about the Roman Empire? The
soldiers, the officers, the generals, even Odoacer himself, were
all Germanic. It was time to make an end of the pretence that
there was still a "Roman" Empire in the West (in the East, in
Constantinople, there was still something like an Empire).

Odoacer went to young Romulus Augustulus and said:
"There is no sense any longer in pretending that you are my
master, or that you, a little boy, are the Emperor, the ruler, of the
Western Empire. I want you to declare that you are giving up the
rulership, and that there is no Emperor of Rome any longer. I
am a Christian, I will not harm you as I easily could. You will be
given a splendid villa and servants who will faithfully look after
you, but as a private citizen."

The boy could do nothing but obey. He gave up the title
"Emperor" and went to live in the villa Odoacer gave him. And
so the Roman Empire, the empire of Augustus, of Nero and
Hadrian, came to an end in AD 476. Roman history began 752
BC and ended 1228 years later in AD 476.

Odoacer could have called himself Emperor, but he had no
wish to have a Roman title that was only an empty word. He had
the power, his Germanic legions obeyed him, and that was all
that mattered to him. It was Odoacer who ended the Roman
Empire in the West, though it had been a pretence for a long
time before.

Many years later there was another invasion of Germanic
tribes from another branch of the Goths, and Odoacer was
killed by the King of the Goths who, for a time, became masters
of Italy.

The whole of Europe was now in the hands of Germanic
tribes who fought each other, and some of whose kingdoms
arose and disappeared within a short time. The Roman Empire
had ceased to exist, but it had left one great legacy: Christianity.

# 54. Angles and Saxons

The Goths under Alaric and the Huns under Attila had shaken the Roman Empire like an earthquake, and as a building comes crumbling down in an earthquake so the whole structure of the Roman Empire came crumbling down. Odoacer then ended it altogether. Only in the East, in Constantinople at least a part of the Roman Empire remained. In the West the Germanic tribes moved in.

Turning to Britain, the Celtic people had become Roman-ised, they had taken Roman customs and used the Latin language and in time they had become Christian. Only north of Hadrian's Wall, the Picts and Scots who were never conquered by Rome, remained pagan, while south of the Wall the people had become Christian and Romans.

When Alaric and his Goths were marching into Italy, Rome decided that the legions in far away Britain were needed more urgently in Italy; Rome could not spare soldiers to defend Britain, it needed them to defend itself. And so one legion after another departed, and Britain was left to fend for herself.

Three hundred years earlier, in the times of Caractacus and Boadicea, the Britons had been warlike people and brave warriors. But in the meantime the Britons had lived the comfortable life of the Romans, if any fighting was to be done it was done by mercenaries who did it for money and for a piece of land. The Britons were no longer used to fighting for themselves, and when the last of the legionaries had left there was no longer an army to defend Britain.

Once the legionaries had gone, the Picts and Scots came raiding across Hadrian's Wall, plundering as they pleased and taking one town in the north after another.

After the Romans had left, England once again became a land of many small kingdoms. And one of these kings, Vortigern of

Kent, thought of a way to protect his land against the wild Picts and Scots: had not the Romans used Germanic tribes to protect their frontiers? The Britons could do as the Romans had done.

And so King Vortigern sent messengers to two Germanic tribes, the Angles and the Saxons who at that time lived on the north coast of Germany. They were promised rich rewards and land in Britain if they came and drove the Picts and Scots back to the forests in the north.

Now among the Angles and Saxons there were many chieftains or Kings, each one ruling a few thousand men. Like all Germanic tribes, most of these kings wanted to move south, and eventually, they did (there is still a part of Germany called Saxony). But two kings accepted the invitation to come to Britain. The names of these two kings may sound strange, but among these Germanic tribes the horse was regarded as the animal of Odin, the wisest of the gods; the horse was for them the animal of wisdom, of cleverness, and to be called "a horse" was a great honour. One of these two kings was called Hengist which meant "stallion," and the other king was called Horsa, "horse."

And these two kings, Hengist and Horsa set out with their followers to Britain. They sailed across the North Sea in their long boats, and arrived in Kent, where the white chalk-cliffs are pounded by the waves of the Channel. The Britons were overjoyed to see these stalwart warriors, thinking their troubles were over. "It is true," said the Britons, "these Angles and Saxons are only pagans, they worship Odin and Thor, but even pagans can be useful."

And they were useful, for the Angles and Saxons kept their part of the bargain and fought the Picts and the Scots driving them back to the North where they had come from. When this was done Hengist and Horsa came to the King of Kent, King Vortigern, for their reward. The British King said: "I have promised you land and I always keep a promise. Tell me how much land do you want?"

And Hengist answered: "Oh, we don't want much, let's say as much land as goes inside a cowhide."

"That's very little indeed," exclaimed the astonished King, "but if that is all you want, you are welcome to it."

But not for nothing had Hengist and Horsa been named after the animals of wisdom. They took a cowhide and cut it into a very thin strip, and when this strip was laid out in a circle it enclosed much more land than King Vortigern had ever thought of giving to them. He was not at all pleased about the trick the cunning Angles and Saxons had played on him, but he could do nothing against it, for he had given his word.

But this was not the end of the story: it was only the beginning. The Angles and Saxons had seen that the Britons were not warriors. It did not take long before the Angles and Saxons attacked the Britons, who realised too late that the "helpers" they had invited were much worse than the Picts and Scots.

The Angles and Saxons not only defeated the Britons in battle, they stormed the cities and towns and burnt them and destroyed them. The Angles and Saxons had no use for cities, for town-life, they loved the free countryside. They destroyed the churches and killed the priests, for the Angles and Saxons were pagans and had no use for churches.

One after another, the Roman-British cities were destroyed, the Britons were killed or sold as slaves, and all the Roman civilisation in Britain, with its the villas and temples, theatres and baths, came to an end. And with the destruction of the churches the Christian religion in Britain also came to an end.

Britain became a pagan land again. In the south the Angles and Saxons were the masters, in the North the Picts and Scots ruled from the forests and mountains.

Only in the mountains of Wales was a small part of Britain where the Christian faith survived. The Angles and Saxons could not conquer Wales and a small number of Britons escaped to Wales and though they built no more Roman cities there, they kept the Christian faith alive. In Ireland, too, the Christian Church lived on. But apart from Ireland and a part of Wales, Britain was again in the hands of barbarians.

The South of Britain became known as Angles-Land, England. There is still a part of England today called East Anglia, that was a separate kingdom of the Angles. Other kingdoms were called East-Sax, West-Sax, South-Sax, which became in time Essex, Wessex, Sussex.

But in contrast to their destructive side, the Angles and Saxons were excellent farmers. They destroyed cities for which they had no use, but they worked the land better than the Britons, for they began to cut down the dense forests of Britain to open the land for farming. The disappearance of the forests in time changed the landscape and life in Britain completely.

# 55. The Bishop of Rome

The whole of Europe was changed by the migration of the peoples, by these Germanic tribes who destroyed the Roman Empire. From the ruins of the Roman Empire there emerged very slowly, the nations and countries as we know them today.

For instance, Gaul, the land which Caesar had conquered for Rome, was invaded by a Germanic tribe called the Franks who settled there. The land of the Franks became France.

The Angles and Saxons at first burnt down cities and killed the Britons, but then settled down and became farmers who tended their land. But there were other Germanic tribes still roving on land and on sea, and some roving bands would suddenly appear on the coast of England, raid villages, plunder what they could, kill the old people and take the younger ones to be sold as slaves.

The Angles and Saxons were no longer on the move; they had found good land and they wanted to live in peace as farmers, but other Germanic tribes were still roaming and pillaging the villages of the Angles and Saxons. Very often children were taken by these pirates and sold to slave-dealers. In those days, fifteen hundred years ago, slave-dealers bought prisoners – men, women and children – from these raiders and pirates and then sold these unhappy people in the market-place of different cities.

One day some English children from the tribe of the Angles were offered for sale in a market-place in Rome. Blue-eyed and fair-haired, they were quite different from the other slaves who were for sale. A Christian priest whose name was Gregory passed by, and looking at that group of children and he thought, "How beautiful these little ones are; it is a sad thing that I am only a poor priest and cannot buy them their freedom, but I must find out where they come from." He turned to the slave-dealer and said: "These are lovely children. What nation has such good-looking boys and girls?"

The slave-dealer answered: "They are Angles, good father."

"Angles?" said Gregory, the priest. "No, they should not be called Angles, they should be called angels."

The slave-dealer laughed, "The tribe from which these children came are far from being angels, they are pagans on the island of Britain."

"Then they should receive the light of Christ," answered Gregory, "and I vow that one day, they will."

He could do nothing for these fair children, but Gregory never forgot them, often thinking of these tribes of Britain who still followed the pagan religion of Odin and Thor, the gods of Valhalla.

But great changes came in the life of Gregory. Not only was he a very good priest, but he was also a very clever man. The people of Rome and his fellow-priests held him in great respect, and in time he became Bishop of Rome.

It was a bad time for Rome when Gregory became Bishop: three-quarters of the city lay in ruins; and among the people who still lived in Rome there was sickness and hunger. In Italy as a whole things were not much better: in the North of Italy another Germanic tribe, the Lombards ("Long Beards") had appeared and had made themselves master. In the South some Germanic tribes had settled but fought each other.

In this hard situation Gregory decided he could not merely remain a bishop, a priest who was only concerned with holding services in a church. He took over the government of Rome, he saw to it that food was brought from the country to Rome, that new and better houses were built. And so slowly a new Rome began to grow, a city of Rome ruled by its bishop.

In time Gregory became so respected that the bishops of other cities, of Ravenna and Naples, accepted him as head of the whole Church, or Pope as it was called (which means "father"). From the time of Gregory onwards the Bishop of Rome was also the ruler of Rome, and head of all bishops, priests and monks.

Rome, which had been the city of the Caesars, began a new life as the city of the Pope, and the centre of all servants of the

Church. Monks, abbots, bishops anywhere in the Western
Roman Empire obeyed the Pope in Rome. But the Eastern
Empire of Constantinople did not. The Church of the East did
not accept the leadership of the Pope in Rome.

But when Gregory the Great (as he came to be called) had
established himself as Pope, as the head of all priests and monks,
he remembered the fair children of the Angles whom he had
called angels. At his command forty monks were sent to Britain
to convert the Angles and Saxons to the Christian religion.

The leader of these monks was called Augustine; he and his
fellow monks were not at all happy to be sent to this wild country in the North: they had heard tales that Britain was a land of
ghosts condemned to hell for their sins, they had heard tales that
the Angles and Saxons ate their enemy's hearts, and that no
human being could learn their horrible language, English. So it
was only because they had sworn obedience that Augustine and
his fellow monks went to Britain by order of Gregory the Great.

But, in fact, things went for them much better than they had
expected. The meeting with the King of the Angles, Ethelbert,
was really a wonderful event. Sitting under a tree, surrounded
by warriors, the King watched the Roman monks coming
towards him, carrying a great silver cross and singing a hymn.
He rose and received the foreigners with friendly words. He
gave them permission to preach their religion, and a year later in
AD 597 Ethelbert was baptised and a great number of his warriors with him. Soon other tribes followed, and Christianity
returned to Britain. The first Christian church was built at
Canterbury.

All this had happened because Gregory had seen the fair
children on the slave-market.

The Picts and the Scots were also converted to Christianity.
However, it was not by missionaries sent from Rome that they
were converted, but by Columba who came from Ireland where
the Christian faith had grown independently of Rome.

Augustine converted the Angles and Saxons in the South,
while Columba and his pupils converted the Picts and Scots in
the North.

# 56. Winfred

When it was at the peak of its power, great parts of Europe, Italy, Spain, Greece, Gaul, Britain, had all been united under the Roman Empire under one law, Roman law. While the Roman legions might have been fighting on the frontiers of the Empire, inside the Empire there was Roman peace, upheld by the Roman law, the *Pax Romana*.

There was a common language, Latin, that was spoken from Britain to Egypt; cities were built to a common pattern, the pattern of Rome, and the way of life was the same in Gaul and in Palestine: the Roman way of life. The *Pax Romana* was a great thing under which so many people could live together in peace.

When the Roman Empire fell under the onslaught of the Germanic tribes it was broken up into many kingdoms, and there was very little peace between neighbouring kingdoms. The great *Pax Romana* had gone, Europe was split into new nations, new countries, and the Germanic tribes who inhabited these new countries fought each other.

There was no longer a common law, or anything else that could hold these warring people together. But if these Germanic tribes became Christian, there was at least a hope that this common Christian faith would be a kind of link between them, and would very slowly change things for better.

The kings might fight each other, but if they were both Christian and both respected the head of the Christian Church, the Pope in Rome, they might listen to his advice and settle their quarrel peacefully. So, the spreading of the Christian religion was the only hope that things would change for the better. The old unity of the Roman Empire, of *Pax Romana,* had gone for good, but a new kind of bond, the Church with its centre in Rome might come about.

So when the monks went out to preach the Christian faith to

pagan tribes, it was not only a matter of religion, but something that should work for a better future for the peoples of Europe. The Angles and Saxons, who had first destroyed Christianity, later through Augustine and his monks, converted to Christianity, and soon some of these Anglo-Saxons themselves became Christian priests and monks. Among the Anglo-Saxon monks were some who took upon themselves the task of bringing the Gospel of Christ to the pagan tribes in the heart of Europe. Alone or in little groups, unarmed, these brave men travelled hundreds of miles into the forests of Germany, Switzerland, Austria. The greatest of these Anglo-Saxon monks was Winfred, or Wynfrith.

In the history books Winfred is usually called by his Latin name, Bonifacius, or Boniface. Since he was not a Roman but an Anglo-Saxon we shall call him by the name he had among his own people.

When Winfred set out, several other missionaries who had gone before him had been cruelly murdered by pagan tribes. But this news could not frighten Winfred. Alone and unarmed he left England and made his way through the forests of Germany.

There was one place which many Germanic tribes regarded as a holy, sacred place. It was a hill which had been cleared of all trees, except one – an enormous, old oak tree. This oak-tree was sacred to Thor, the god of thunder and lightning. And no man would have dared to touch this tree for it was said that anyone who touched the tree would be killed immediately by a stroke of lightning. But at certain times the pagan tribes came together on that hill and worshipped Thor and made sacrifices to him.

Winfred waited for such an occasion. And when hundreds of warriors had come to the hill and stood in a big circle around the holy oak tree, Winfred walked into the circle, carrying a large axe. While all the men stared at him with surprise Winfred walked up to the tree, lifted the axe and drove it deeply into the wood.

The warriors stood aghast: they expected a bolt of lightning to strike, but nothing happened. Winfred kept striking the tree and his axe bit deeper and deeper into the wood. The tribesmen became alarmed, looking for someone to stop this man. But before they could act, the mighty tree swayed and came crashing down. While the tribesmen stared with horror at the tree of Thor lying on the ground, Winfred cried out: "See how powerless your gods are! Turn to the true God!"

Then he walked away. Not a man would have dared to lift a hand against him. From that day onwards more and more warriors came to him to be instructed in the Christian religion and to be baptised. With the help of these new Christians Winfred built a church on the hill of Thor from the wood of Thor's oak tree.

For thirty years Winfred, or Boniface, lived among the tribes in Germany and converted many of them to Christianity. When he was already an old man he set out with some friends to convert a tribe in the North of Germany, the Frisians. But the Frisians had heard of Winfred: they did not want to have their way of life changed by this Christian religion and they came with drawn swords against Winfred and his companions. Winfred's friends drew their swords to defend him, but he said: "No. We must not shed any blood to defend ourselves – Christ Himself did not do so."

He and his companions were killed; they died for their faith. Yet through his work and the work of others like him, the Germanic tribes were, in time, converted and became Christian.

So the Angles and Saxons had first destroyed Christianity in Britain. But the fair children sold in the slave-market turned the mind of Gregory to the task of bringing the Christian faith again to Britain. In time, the Anglo-Saxons produced such heroes as Winfred (or Boniface) who carried the message of Christ into the forests of Germany.

# Index

# Other Waldorf Education Resources
## by Charles Kovacs

*Class 4 (age 9–10)*
Norse Mythology

*Classes 4 and 5 (age 9–11)*
The Human Being and the Animal World

*Classes 5 and 6 (age 10–12)*
Ancient Greece
Botany

*Class 6 (age 11–12)*
Ancient Rome

*Classes 6 and 7 (age 11–13)*
Geology and Astronomy

*Class 7 (age 12–13)*
The Age of Discovery

*Classes 7 and 8 (age 12–14)*
Muscles and Bones

*Class 8 (age 13–14)*
The Age of Revolution

*Class 11 (age 16–17)*
Parsifal and the Search for the Grail

*General interest*
The Spiritual Background to Christian Festivals
The Apocalypse in Rudolf Steiner's Lecture Series